Making CONNECTIONS

Intro

Skills and Strategies for Academic Reading

Teacher's Manual

Jessica Williams | David Wiese

CAMBRIDGE
UNIVERSITY PRESS

CAMBRIDGE
UNIVERSITY PRESS

32 Avenue of the Americas, New York NY 10013-2473, USA

Cambridge University Press is part of the University of Cambridge.

It furthers the University's mission by disseminating knowledge in the pursuit of education, learning and research at the highest international levels of excellence.

www.cambridge.org
Information on this title: www.cambridge.org/9781107516076

First published 2016

Printed in Dubai by Oriental Press

A catalogue record for this publication is available from the British Library

ISBN 978-1-107-51607-6 Student's Book
ISBN 978-1-107-51609-0 Teacher's Manual

Additional resources for this publication at www.cambridge.org/makingconnections

Cambridge University Press has no responsibility for the persistence or accuracy of URLs for external or third-party internet websites referred to in this publication, and does not guarantee that any content on such websites is, or will remain, accurate or appropriate. Information regarding prices, travel timetables, and other factual information given in this work is correct at the time of first printing but Cambridge University Press does not guarantee the accuracy of such information thereafter.

Contents

Teaching Suggestions

The *Making Connections Intro* Student's Book consists of eight units, each of which is organized in the following way:

- Two Skills and Strategies sections alternate with the readings. The first precedes Readings 1 and 2, and the second precedes Reading 3. These sections introduce and practice specific skills and strategies for reading.
- The three readings are each accompanied by associated activities in reading and vocabulary development. The final reading is the longest and most challenging.
- A final section, Making Connections, provides two cohesion-building exercises.

Students at the high beginning level and above need to expand their vocabulary in order to prepare for academic courses. Strategies and activities to help students expand their vocabulary are therefore important features of *Making Connections Intro*. The post-reading activities following each of the three readings in a unit include tasks that facilitate vocabulary expansion by focusing on 16 vocabulary items used in the reading. Additionally, tasks for vocabulary from the Academic Word List (AWL) follow the final reading. All vocabulary items are listed and defined, with an example provided, in Appendix 1 of the Student's Book (pages 257–267). In Appendix 2 of the Student's Book (pages 268–269), each key vocabulary item is indexed by the unit and the reading in which it is first used. The 🅐 icon indicates vocabulary items from the AWL.

Making Connections Intro has enough material for a reading course of 50 to 70 class hours, assuming a corresponding number of hours are available for homework assignments. Completing all the Beyond the Reading activities that accompany each reading might make the course longer.

Skills, strategies, and vocabulary are recycled within a unit and in subsequent units. It is recommended, therefore, that in planning a course outline, the order of the book be followed.

Skills and Strategies

The Skills and Strategies sections introduce reading and vocabulary-building strategies that are then incorporated into the reading activities.

Rationale

Research suggests that good readers apply various strategies when they are reading a text. The Skills and Strategies sections introduce and provide practice with a variety of these reading strategies.

Description

The first Skills and Strategies section of each unit introduces vocabulary-building skills and strategies: finding the meaning of words, noticing parts of words, and using learner dictionaries. The second Skills and Strategies section in each unit focuses on reading strategies: finding the topic, main ideas and supporting details and finding steps in a process, advantages and disadvantages, causes and effects, and problems and solutions.

Each Skills and Strategies section provides two to three Skill Practice activities that move students from recognition to production. More practice in each skill is provided in the While You Read section. Students then review each skill and strategy within the Skill Review section. Strategies are recycled throughout the text.

How to Use

The Skills and Strategies sections are best introduced in class, supported by the use of other materials (e.g., examples similar to those in the Examples & Explanations subsection). At the beginning of the course, each of the Skill Practice activities should be partially completed in class. Then, when you are confident that your students understand the form and content of each activity, an appropriate number of items can be assigned for homework.

Before You Read

Connecting to the Topic

Rationale

The purpose of this activity is to get students to activate background knowledge relevant to the content of the reading that follows. Effective reading occurs when readers are able to place new information within the context of information they already possess.

Description

This is the first of two activities that occur before each reading. It consists of questions for discussion with a partner.

How to Use

This activity can be introduced through short, full-class discussions. Partners or small groups can then continue the discussions.

Previewing and Predicting

Rationale

The purpose of this activity is to get students into the habit of previewing the content and organization of a text before they start reading in depth. Previewing has been shown to be a key strategy that enhances a reader's ability to understand a text on first encounter.

Description

Making Connections Intro uses different techniques for previewing texts. Students are taught to look at titles, headings, pictures, and graphic information such as charts to guess what information might appear, or to form questions that they expect a reading to answer. Each technique encourages the student to interact with the text before beginning to read for deeper understanding.

How to Use

These activities are best introduced, modeled, and practiced in class. We recommend that students first work with a partner. The primary goal of this activity is to encourage active interaction with the text.

While You Read

Rationale

Research suggests that good readers read actively by asking themselves questions and monitoring comprehension as they read. The While You Read tasks encourage students to adopt this approach. These tasks focus students' attention on the strategic nature of the reading process during their first read-through of a text. These tasks appear in the margins of the text and force students to stop and apply the strategies presented in the earlier Skills and Strategies sections. Students are thus encouraged to do what good readers do – to interact with the text while they read.

Description

While You Read boxes are in the margin of every reading, opposite some words in bold blue within a line of text. Students are directed to stop reading at the end of the sentence containing the bold blue text and to perform a strategic task designed to support effective reading.

While You Read provides practice for the skills and strategies previously introduced. It reinforces lexical skills by having students identify context clues to meaning, figure out a word's part of speech, look up challenging words in a dictionary, and recognize collocations. It provides practice in reading skills by having students identify main ideas and supporting details and understand connections between paragraphs.

How to Use

While You Read is best introduced and modeled as a classroom activity after the reading has been previewed. We recommend that you first introduce students to the concept of active reading. You can do this by reading the first reading of Unit 1 out loud. As you come to each bold blue word, stop and read the While You Read directions. Answer the question before you continue to read. Note that this technique will be new to many students, particularly those who do not read extensively in their native language. Students will find it a time-consuming process at first, but assure them that, with practice, they will gradually apply these strategies automatically and their reading speed and comprehension will increase.

At first, many of the boxes in the shorter readings can be completed during an initial in-class read-through. This will allow you to provide students with the intensive guidance, practice, and immediate feedback on their performances that they will need as they learn to apply these skills independently.

To help students focus on the reading process, it is strongly recommended that no dictionary be used during this first read-through. We also recommend that the first read-through include reading for main ideas. (See the Main Idea Check section below.)

One challenge in the While You Read activity is that students tend to make excessive use of highlighting and/or underlining. Try to help students understand that highlighting or underlining entire paragraphs, for example, is not an effective reading strategy. In fact, indiscriminate highlighting is a counterproductive activity. To avoid this, have the students follow the directions provided in the Skills and Strategies sections: highlight main ideas only, number supporting details, and underline key vocabulary.

Audio recordings of the readings are available for free download at www.cambridge.org/makingconnections.

Reading Skill Development

Main Idea Check

Rationale

Students often focus too much on the details in a reading rather than on its main ideas. The Main Idea Check activity provides an opportunity for students to focus on an understanding of the main ideas of each paragraph. It is only after students have grasped the main ideas of a reading that they can make sense of how the details fit into this larger frame of meaning.

Description

For Unit 1 and the first two readings of Unit 2, the Main Idea Check asks students to choose from four options the sentence that best expresses the main idea of the entire reading. For the remainder of the readings, the Main Idea Check has students identify the main idea of different paragraphs by matching the paragraph number to the sentence expressing its main idea.

How to Use

Before starting the Main Idea Check tasks in Unit 1, we recommend that you read Skills and Strategies 4 in Unit 2 so that you know the main idea identification strategies that will be explicitly introduced there.

For Unit 1, and Readings 1 and 2 in Unit 2, use a simple approach with which you are comfortable, without going into the issue in any great detail. It would be helpful, for

example, to have students discuss why the other choices do not represent the main idea of the reading.

After you work through the strategy-based approach to main idea identification in Skills and Strategies 4, the Main Idea Check tasks may be assigned for work in class or for homework. In classes with additional writing goals, students could be asked to rewrite the sentences of the Main Idea Check tasks in their own words and then put the sentences together to form a summary of the given reading.

A Closer Look

Rationale

Having understood the main ideas in a reading, students need to achieve a more in-depth understanding of it. In this activity, therefore, students are asked to go back to the reading and read for details and to establish connections among them.

Description

Many of the questions in A Closer Look are types of questions with which students will probably be familiar (e.g., true/false and multiple choice). We recommend that early on in the text, perhaps in Unit 2, you review some common strategies in answering multiple-choice questions. You can encourage students to use the following strategies:

- Read the directions very carefully.
- Read all the possible answers before choosing the correct one.
- Eliminate the obviously incorrect answers.
- Recognize that a wrong answer may include an incorrect fact or information not in the reading.
- Recognize that all information within the answer must be true for the answer to be correct.

You should also alert students to one question type that is possibly less familiar. To encourage the synthesizing of information, a significant number of multiple-choice questions have more than one correct answer. In these questions, students are instructed as to how many answers they should choose.

How to Use

Generally, the tasks in A Closer Look lend themselves well to completion outside of class. However, we suggest that at first you give students some classroom practice in answering this section.

A useful tool for students as they complete A Closer Look tasks is Appendix 1, Key Vocabulary (pages 257–267 in the Student's Book). This appendix lists the vocabulary alphabetically within each reading, thus providing accessible and convenient support for students during these more detailed examinations of the readings. For more information on Appendix 1, see page 7 of this Teacher's Manual.

Skill Review

Rationale

Students need multiple opportunities to practice new reading and vocabulary-building skills and strategies. This is particularly important as new skills are introduced that build upon understanding of those previously taught.

Description

The Skill Review allows students to practice specific skills introduced in the Skills and Strategies sections. The content reflects the previous reading and therefore should be sufficiently familiar to enable students to focus on the skill itself.

How to Use

This is a good homework assignment. Students can then compare their work in small groups. If students encounter problems with this task, direct them back to the appropriate Skills and Strategies section. It is worth taking the time in class to really explain these tasks since they are key to academic reading.

Vocabulary Development

Definitions

Rationale

This activity provides a simple and structured way for students to take their first steps in learning the target vocabulary in each of the 24 readings.

Description

In this activity, students find a word in the reading that is similar in meaning to each of eight given definitions. This is a simple way for students to focus on target vocabulary in context without having to use bilingual dictionaries. Part-of-speech information about the target vocabulary has been provided so that students can integrate this information into the vocabulary-learning process.

How to Use

This activity is best introduced as a classroom activity. It can then be completed either in or out of class as homework.

Words in Context

Rationale

Understanding the meaning of unknown target words by perceiving the surrounding context of the word has been demonstrated to be an important skill in vocabulary acquisition. This activity helps students to see the linguistic contexts in which the target words belong.

Description

There are three types of Words in Context activities: fill-in-the-blank within sentences, fill-in-the blanks within paragraphs, and matching. All activities introduce words or phrases from the readings that have not been targeted in the preceding Definitions exercise. The key vocabulary items are presented at the beginning of the activity.

How to Use

This activity can be completed either in or out of class. Encourage students to go back to the reading and find the target words if they cannot readily answer the questions. Although these words are recycled in later readings, we encourage you to expand this practice by creating vocabulary tests focusing on these target words. Testing students on some of the vocabulary from Unit 1 while they are working on later units, for example, will help them to retain vocabulary.

Word Families

Rationale

High-beginning–level learners need to build their academic vocabulary quickly in order to be successful in more advanced courses. Recognizing different word forms allows students to increase their receptive vocabulary quickly and efficiently. By focusing on parts of speech, this approach to vocabulary building also may help students move toward the ability to use the vocabulary in writing and speech.

Description

This activity displays related noun and verb forms in a table. The boldface word in each table is the part of speech that appears in the reading. Students are instructed to locate the words in the reading and use context clues to figure out the meanings. If the students are still unsure, you may direct them to Appendix 1 on page 257 to check the meaning of unfamiliar vocabulary. Students choose the correct word form to complete the ten fill-in-the-blank sentences.

How to Use

We recommend that you introduce this activity in class, as students may need more instruction in parts of speech. They may also need guidance in using the correct form of the word.

Academic Word List

Rationale

The Academic Word List (Coxhead, 2000) provides a corpus of the most frequently used academic words. *Making Connections Intro* provides students with the opportunity to learn this vocabulary, an activity key to preparing for academic coursework in all fields of study.

Description

After the final reading, this fill-in-the-blank activity focuses on AWL vocabulary items from the two preceding readings.

How to Use

Before you begin this activity, it is important to explain the significance of general academic vocabulary. Make sure that students know AWL items are not technical, subject-specific terms but rather general words common to all academic coursework. Research has shown that students need familiarity with this vocabulary in order to understand college texts.

The Academic Word List activity provides an opportunity for students to go back to the readings and explore vocabulary if needed. This can be done out of class, but it also works well as a group activity with students discussing possible answers and referring to the readings to explain their choices. It is recommended that students learn this vocabulary by making word cards.

Beyond the Reading

Critical Thinking

Rationale

A successful college student does not merely accumulate information. Rather, that student engages in thoughtful, reflective, and independent thinking in order to make sense of a text. Critical thinking skills enable a student to evaluate what they read, make connections, ask questions, solve problems, and apply that information to new situations.

Description

Each Critical Thinking activity defines a specific critical thinking skill and then allows students to practice that skill in a context linked to the previous reading. Examples of specific skills include clarifying concepts, applying information to new situations, and offering opinions.

How to Use

Before you begin this activity, it is a good idea to discuss the difference between memorization and comprehension. Introduce critical thinking skills as an essential part of comprehension. This is particularly important as some students may come from educational systems that emphasize rote learning rather than critical thinking. The activity itself could be assigned to in-class groups, or as homework. The latter would allow a student to spend time exploring the specific critical thinking skill. Students could then compare their responses in groups.

Research

Rationale

Some teachers may want to use the readings as an opportunity for their students to undertake some research on the topics of the readings.

Description

This activity occurs after each of the 24 readings. It offers topics for students to research and discuss that are relevant to the subject of a reading.

How to Use

The research questions offer opportunities for students to tackle more challenging reading tasks as well as to pursue more personally stimulating aspects of a given topic. Some of the research requires students to do self-reflection or survey classmates to gather more data. Some require students to go online to find additional information.

Writing

Rationale

Students develop deeper understanding of a reading and become more adept in using new vocabulary if provided an opportunity to reflect and write about what they have read.

Description

This writing activity appears at the close of each reading. It allows students to use their discussion and research activity as the basis to write short paragraphs.

How to Use

The paragraphs can be produced in or outside of class. Remind students to use information from their research activity within their writing. It is also a good idea to encourage them to use new vocabulary they have learned from that unit.

Improving Your Reading Speed

Rationale

Slow reading is a common complaint of second-language learners. It is frustrating, and it impedes comprehension. While individuals will read at different rates, gradually increasing rates for all students will allow students to read more effectively and with more pleasure and confidence.

Description

This activity appears at the end of unit. Students are directed to choose one of the previous readings within the unit and time themselves as they read. They then record their time in a chart in Appendix 3 on pages 271–272. This practice provides the opportunity for students to see their reading speed improve as they practice.

How to Use

We do not recommend that teachers suggest an ideal words-per-minute reading rate for two reasons. First, students will read at different rates. Equally important, good readers vary their rate according to a text and reading purpose. Instead, focus on improving individual rates while stressing that effective reading involves both adequate speed and comprehension.

Have students read Appendix 3 before they complete this activity. This will allow them to learn and practice strategies that will improve their reading rates. It is also important that students identify personal reading habits, such as reading out loud or looking at each individual word, that slow down reading rates.

It is a good idea to complete this activity in class the first time. You might need to help students compute their words-per-minute rates and enter these in their charts. Most of all, stress that, like any skill, improving reading speed requires practice.

Making Connections

As the final review activity of each unit, two exercises give students practice in establishing within short texts the cohesion of vocabulary, structural features, and organizational patterns.

Rationale

These tasks provide students with a focused opportunity to practice reading for cohesion between sentences and short paragraphs. In addition, students get a further opportunity to review recently targeted academic vocabulary.

Description

Units 1 to 7 introduce and give students practice with strategies writers use to achieve cohesion:

- Use of pronoun and antecedent connectors
- Connectors that signal categories
- Connectors that signal additional information
- Connectors that signal sequence
- Connectors that signal contrast
- Connectors that signal cause and effect

Unit 8 allows students to review and apply all six strategies. Practice begins at the sentence level and progresses to short paragraphs. Target vocabulary from the unit is recycled throughout this Making Connections section.

How to Use

This section is probably best performed in class, where fairly immediate feedback is available. Students can work individually or in pairs. Feedback may be supplied by you and/or elicited from students. You can expand this practice by presenting other jigsaw-type activities. For example, use a paragraph that has the same cohesion-building strategies.

Appendices

Appendix 1: Key Vocabulary
(pages 257–267)

Appendix 1 is the "dictionary" for *Making Connections Intro*. For each reading, the target vocabulary items are listed alphabetically, defined simply and clearly, and exemplified in a sentence. The dictionary's purpose is to offer students easy access to information on the meaning and use of each word during the vocabulary learning process, especially while they are completing the Vocabulary Development activities. It can also be used during students' work on A Closer Look. Note that vocabulary from the AWL is indicated by the Ⓐ icon.

Appendix 2: Index to Key Vocabulary
(pages 268–269)

Appendix 2 is an index that lists each key vocabulary item by the unit and the reading in which it is first introduced, thus allowing students to locate the original dictionary entry for a vocabulary item when necessary.

Note that vocabulary from the AWL is indicated by the Ⓐ icon.

Appendix 3: Improving Your Reading Speed (pages 270–272)

Appendix 3 begins with a list of strategies students can employ in order to improve their reading speed. It is a good idea to discuss these strategies before students practice this skill. It also includes a chart that students will use to record their reading rates as they work through the Student's Book.

Answer Key

Human Behavior

Skills and Strategies 1
Finding the Meanings of Words: Definitions

Skill Practice 1 *Page 3*

2. means
3. This
4. in other words
5. ( )
6. – –
7. that is
8. these

Skill Practice 2 *Page 4*

2. the feeling of having too many things to do
3. a list of the student's tasks and problems along with the date or time to deal with each one
4. without wasting time
5. finish
6. say something strongly and often
7. very tired
8. their marks on tests and exams

Reading 1
Procrastination

Connecting to the Topic *Page 5*

Answers will vary.

Previewing and Predicting *Page 5*

b, c, f

While You Read *Page 5*

1. a) good
2. a) good idea

Reading Skill Development

Main Idea Check *Page 8*

b

A Closer Look *Page 8*

1. b, c
2. True
3. c
4. a
5. b

Skill Review *Page 9*

A

WORD	THAT IS + DEFINITION	MEANS + DEFINITION IS + DEFINITION	PUNCTUATION
procrastination (*n*) Par. 2		✓	
postponing (*v*) Par. 2			✓
pleasant (*adj*) Par. 2	✓		
meet a deadline (*v*) Par. 2		✓	
consider (*v*) Par. 4			✓
set priorities (*n*) Par. 4	✓		

B

WORD	DEFINITION
procrastination (*n*) Par. 2	postponing tasks that you should do now until some time in the future
postponing (*v*) Par. 2	delaying
pleasant (*adj*) Par. 2	enjoy[able]
meet a deadline (*v*) Par. 2	completing a task by the time it needs to be done
consider (*v*) Par. 4	really think about (it) hard
set priorities (*n*) Par. 4	decide which things are more important and which things are less important

Vocabulary Development

Definitions *Page 10*

1. Tasks
2. postpone (or delay)
3. factor
4. prefer
5. deadline
6. positive
7. perspective
8. expert

Words in Context *Page 10*

1. bill
2. assignment
3. leaning
4. guilty
5. accomplish
6. repair
7. put off
8. due

Reading 2
Memory and New Technology

Connecting to the Topic *Page 12*
Answers will vary.

Previewing and Predicting *Page 12*
a, b, e, f

While You Read *Page 12*
1. means "the ability to remember facts, events, and people."
2. – a small museum

Reading Skill Development

Main Idea Check *Page 15*
a

A Closer Look *Page 15*
1. b, d
2. Group 1: a, b
   Group 2: c
3. b, –; e, +
4. False
5. d
6. True

Skill Review *Page 16*
A

WORD OR PHRASE	SAME SENTENCE	NEXT SENTENCE
author (*n*) Par. 1	✓	
memory (*n*) Par. 1	✓	
experiment (*n*) Par. 3	✓	
gallery (*n*) Par. 5	✓	

B

WORD OR PHRASE	DEFINITION
author (*n*) Par. 1	writer
memory (*n*) Par. 1	the ability to remember facts, events, and people
experiment (*n*) Par. 3	a scientific study
gallery (*n*) Par. 5	a small museum

Vocabulary Development

Definitions *Page 17*
1. instant
2. store
3. stress
4. negative
5. impact
6. affect
7. *Visual*
8. recent

Word Families *Page 17*
1. consultation
2. support
3. access
4. advice
5. consult
6. preservation
7. support
8. advise
9. access
10. preserve

Skills and Strategies 2
Finding the Topic of a Paragraph

Skill Practice 1 *Page 21*
1. b
2. c
3. a
4. c

Skill Practice 2 *Page 22*
1. Honest Tea
2. an experiment
3. results

Reading 3
Lying

Connecting to the Topic *Page 23*
Answers will vary.

Previewing and Predicting *Page 23*

SECTION	TOPIC
II	A professor who studies lies
III	What makes people lie more
III	What makes people lie less
I	Why people lie
I	Why lying is sometimes easier than telling the truth

While You Read *Page 23*
1. – that they are not so important
2. Probably because lying is very useful, so useful that we are willing to break our own rules.
3. Some conditions did affect the amount of lying, however.

Reading Skill Development

Main Idea Check *Page 26*
b, c

A Closer Look *Page 26*

1. True
2. a, b, d
3. c
4. d
5. a
6. False
7. a, c

Skill Review *Page 27*

A

1. reason(s), protect
2. condition(s) / money

B

1. 5
2. 2
3. 4
4. 6
5. 7
6. 3

Vocabulary Development

Definitions *Page 28*

1. gap
2. image
3. avoid
4. maintain
5. Research
6. Participants
7. reward
8. significantly

Words in Context *Page 28*

1. punishment
2. rude
3. detect
4. benefit
5. probability
6. sum
7. logical
8. primary

Academic Word List *Page 29*

1. stressed
2. participants
3. research
4. significantly
5. access
6. detect
7. expert
8. perspective
9. factor
10. positive

Making Connections

Exercise 1 *Page 31*

2. Every year, there is a <u>World Memory Championship</u>. People come from all over the world to participate in it.

3. <u>Dominic O'Brien</u> won the first championship in 1991. He won again the next year it was held in 1993, but another person beat him in 1994.

4. <u>O'Brien</u> won the Championship several more times. His record remains the best.

5. In 2011, <u>a 21-year-old Chinese</u> won the championship. He listened to <u>400 numbers</u> and remembered 300 of them.

6. You may not have a good <u>memory</u> now. However, if you practice, you can improve it and perhaps participate in the championship next year.

Exercise 2 *Page 32*

1. CBA
2. CAB
3. ABC
4. CBA
5. BAC

2 Fact or Fiction

Skills and Strategies 3
Finding the Meanings of Words:
Examples

Skill Practice 1 *Page 35*

2. the heart and brain
3. chicken soup, orange juice, and extra sleep
4. fruits, nuts, and vegetables
5. important exams, presentations, and job interviews
6. hot red peppers
7. talk about our problems at work or in marriage
8. "don't do this," "be careful about that," or "that's bad for you."

Skill Practice 2 *Page 35*
Answers will vary. Suggested answers:

2. parts of the body with a special purpose
3. something you do to cure an illness or medical problem
4. healthy; relating to food that is good for your body
5. making you worry a lot
6. having a strong, hot taste
7. say that something is wrong or that you are annoyed about something
8. tell someone that something bad may happen in the future

Reading 1
Fact or Fiction – Science

Connecting to the Topic *Page 37*
Answers will vary.

Previewing and Predicting *Page 37*
3, 6

While You Read *Page 37*

1. like a penny
2. that is, common beliefs that are actually false
3. b

Reading Skill Development

Main Idea Check *Page 40*
d

A Closer Look *Page 40*

1. a, c, d
2. False
3. True
4. c
5. a
6. b

Skill Review *Page 41*

1. E, If you drop a **coin**, like a penny, from a very tall building, you could kill a person who is standing below.
2. D, They are all science **myths**, that is, common beliefs that are actually false.
3. D, In fact, there is no **evidence** – no supporting facts – for any of these beliefs.
4. E, This idea first appeared in a book about **outdoor sports**, like swimming and boating, in 1908.
5. E, Most of these ideas originated when very little was known about health or **diseases**, such as measles, or the flu, or even colds.

Vocabulary Development

Definitions *Page 42*

1. twice
2. abandon
3. persist
4. generation
5. virus
6. drown
7. relevant
8. beneficial

Words in Context *Page 42*

1. familiar
2. lightning
3. originated
4. Repetition
5. immediately
6. evidence
7. fingernails
8. resist

Reading 2
Fact or Fiction – History

Connecting to the Topic *Page 44*
Answers will vary.

Previewing and Predicting *Page 44*

1. M
2. T
3. F
4. M
5. F

While You Read *Page 44*

1. like spaghetti
2. So, why do we often give Marco Polo credit for spaghetti?
3. for example, how to grow rice, beans, and fruit.

Reading Skill Development

Main Idea Check *Page 47*

b

A Closer Look *Page 47*

1. False
2. a
3. False
4. d
5. True
6. False
7. b, d, e

Skill Review *Page 48*

A

WORD OR PHRASE	DEFINITION	EXAMPLE	CLUE
fiction (Par. 1)	✓		that is
pasta (Par. 3)		✓	like
the New World (Par. 5)	✓		punctuation
agriculture (Par. 8)	✓		which is
asp (Par. 8)	✓		punctuation

B

Word	Examples
pasta	spaghetti

Vocabulary Development

Definitions *Page 49*

1. make up
2. publish
3. handsome
4. prove
5. Spices
6. widespread
7. trace
8. Astronauts

Words in Context *Page 49*

1. established
2. ancient
3. Traders
4. culture
5. explorer
6. credit
7. voyage
8. historians

Skills and Strategies 4
Finding the Main Idea of a Paragraph

Skill Practice 1 *Page 52*

1. a
2. b
3. a
4. a

Skill Practice 2 *Page 53*

1. Some people try to fight email scammers.
2. People try to fight email scammers for different reasons.
3. There are several ways to fight email scammers.
4. You need to be careful when you fight email scammers.

Reading 3
Hoaxes

Connecting to the Topic *Page 54*
Answers will vary.

Previewing and Predicting *Page 54*

SECTION	TOPIC
I and II	Famous hoaxes
I	An example of a hoax that made money
I and II	Reasons for hoaxes
II	An example of a hoax that was not for money
I and II	Why people believe hoaxes

While You Read *Page 54*

1. In other words, the person who creates a hoax is trying to trick people.
2. b
3. – a creature with the body of a human and the tail of a fish
4. b

Reading Skill Development

Main Idea Check *Page 57*

A 3
B 5
C 2

D 1
E 4

A Closer Look *Page 57*

1. False
2. a, c
3. c
4. b
5. a H, b H, c T, d H, e T, f T, g H
6. c
7. True
8. b

Skill Review *Page 58*

A

PARAGRAPH NUMBER	WHAT IS THE PARAGRAPH ABOUT?	WHAT DOES THE WRITER WANT TO SAY ABOUT IT?
1	An introduction to hoaxes	A hoax is an intentional deception, but lots of people believe them.
2	An example that illustrates one reason for hoaxes	The Tasaday is an example of a hoax that was created for fame and profit.
3	The discovery of a hoax	A lot of clues suggested that the story of the Tasaday was a hoax.
4	Other hoaxes for profit	There have been a lot of these through history.
5	An example of another reason for hoaxes	Bigfoot is an example of a hoax that began as a joke.

Vocabulary Development

Definitions *Page 59*

1. profit
2. Caves
3. Tools
4. area
5. contact
6. Curiosity
7. Jokes
8. occur

Word Families *Page 59*

1. assistance
2. deceive
3. reveal
4. collect
5. revelation
6. deception
7. create
8. assist
9. creation
10. collection

Academic Word List *Page 60*

1. generation
2. evidence
3. published
4. beneficial
5. widespread
6. contact
7. persisted
8. established
9. occurred
10. revealed

Making Connections

Exercise 1 *Page 62*

2 Einstein began to speak later than other children. This worried Einstein's parents.

3 People have said that Einstein was bad at math as a child. That is simply not true.

4 Napoleon was about five feet, seven inches (1.7 meters) tall. This was average for the time.

5 British historians say he was only five feet, two inches (1.57 meters) tall. Historians have proven that this is not true.

6 The British and French reports of Napoleon's height were different. This was because the British and French used different systems of measurement.

Exercise 2 *Page 63*

1. BAC
2. CAB
3. ABC
4. BCA
5. CBA

3 Marketing

Skills and Strategies 5
Finding the Meanings of Words: Contrasts

Skill Practice 1 *Page 67*
2. all the time
3. in only a few places
4. old age
5. pay attention
6. low-level worker
7. immediately
8. not getting good results

Skill Practice 2 *Page 68*
Answers will vary. Suggested answers:
2. sometimes, not often
3. in many places
4. young people; the quality of being young
5. pay no attention to
6. a high-level worker in a company; a person who makes important business decisions
7. slowly over a period of time
8. successful; getting good results

Reading 1
How Do Advertisements Work?

Connecting to the Topic *Page 69*
Answers will vary.

Previewing and Predicting *Page 69*
B
b, e

While You Read *Page 69*
1. for example, computers or shoes
2. Advertisements, or "ads," with rational appeals present a logical reason for why you should buy a company's products or use its services.
3. but suddenly, you begin to think that driving it might be dangerous.

Reading Skill Development

Main Idea Check *Page 72*
A 2   D 5
B 4   E 3
C 1

A Closer Look *Page 72*
1. b, d   5. a
2. True   6. b
3. b   7. c
4. d

Skill Review *Page 73*
A
1. Unlike ads with rational appeals, which try to show that a product is effective, ads with **emotional** appeals try to change how you feel.
2. You thought your old car was **safe**, but suddenly, you begin to think that driving it might be dangerous.
3. Perhaps you want to have a life like that. You want that car, too. It may make you feel **envious**. In contrast, an ad that shows a big family enjoying a car trip together might make you feel happy and satisfied.
4. The purpose of ads like these is usually very clear, but other ads are **not so direct**.

B
1. benefits   3. widespread
2. curiosity   4. postpone

Vocabulary Development

Definitions *Page 74*
1. Principles   5. encourage
2. achieve   6. rational
3. goal   7. effective
4. Customers   8. figure

Word Families *Page 74*
1. aware   6. emotion
2. directness   7. direct
3. athlete   8. athletic
4. envious   9. envy
5. awareness   10. emotional

Reading 2
The Psychology of Price

Connecting to the Topic *Page 76*
Answers will vary.

Previewing and Predicting *Page 76*
Some answers will vary.

1. They are about prices.
2. during sales; when customers need to compare prices
3. on a store window; on a menu
4. to help the reader understand the text better
5. 49

While You Read *Page 76*
1. At the heart of most price strategies is a fundamental principle called *the anchor.*
2. but not always
3. The psychology of price is at work in all sorts of places, including on menus.

Reading Skill Development

Main Idea Check *Page 79*
A 3   C 1
B 4   D 2

A Closer Look *Page 79*
1. True   4. False
2. c   5. b
3. d   6. a

Skill Review *Page 80*
A
1. D less than what the product was worth
2. D the first idea you have about how much a product is worth
3. C higher
4. C always
5. E a big steak or lobster
6. E €, $, or ¥

Vocabulary Development

Definitions *Page 81*
1. value   5. bargain
2. fundamental   6. menu
3. anchor   7. item
4. tag   8. symbol

Words in Context *Page 81*
1. reduced   5. trick
2. sign   6. profitable
3. crossed out   7. sale
4. effect   8. designed

Skills and Strategies 6
Finding the Topic and Main Idea of a Reading

Skill Practice 1 *Page 84*
1. b   2. c

Skill Practice 2 *Page 85*
Undercover marketing can be very successful, but it must be done carefully.
Clearly, undercover marketing has both benefits and risks.
Answers will vary. Suggested answers:
Topic of the reading: Undercover marketing
Main idea of the reading: It can be very successful, but it must be done carefully. / It has benefits and risks.

Reading 3
Guerrilla Marketing

Connecting to the Topic *Page 86*
Answers will vary.

Previewing and Predicting *Page 86*
A
1. b   2. b

While You Read *Page 86*
1. One strategy for doing this is *guerrilla marketing*
2. that is, on the Internet
3. c

Reading Skill Development

Main Idea Check *Page 89*
A 3   D 7
B 6   E 2
C 4   F 5

A Closer Look *Page 89*

1. b
2. a, b
3. False
4. c
5. b
6. a
7. a, c

Skill Review *Page 90*

A

guerilla marketing

B

GUERRILLA MARKETING STRATEGY	MAKES PEOPLE AWARE OF THE COMPANY AND ITS PRODUCTS	MAKES PEOPLE LIKE THE COMPANY AND ITS PRODUCTS
Flash mobs	✓	✓
Coke happiness	✓	✓
UNICEF vending machines	✓	✓

C

Guerilla marketing can be effective.

Vocabulary Development

Definitions *Page 92*

1. strategy
2. regular
3. mob
4. perform
5. post
6. Communities
7. promote
8. Professionals

Words in Context *Page 92*

1. f
2. c
3. h
4. a
5. b
6. d
7. e
8. g

Academic Word List *Page 93*

1. strategy
2. symbol
3. similar
4. goal / strategy
5. professionals
6. achieve
7. aware
8. community
9. principles
10. rational

Making Connections

Exercise 1 *Page 95*

2 Some advertisements use <u>musicians, actors or athletes</u>. These famous people can help sell products.

3 <u>A special song</u> can also help sell a product. Customers hear this music in their heads, and they think about the product.

4 In the last five years, there has been a lot of marketing on <u>social media</u>. These sites include Facebook and YouTube.

5 Some companies prefer <u>more traditional ways of marketing</u>. These methods include newspaper and television ads.

6 <u>Direct marketing</u> can be very effective. An example of this kind of advertising is a text message on your cell phone about a special sale.

Exercise 2 *Page 96*

1. ACB
2. BAC
3. CBA
4. ACB
5. BAC

4 Taste

Skills and Strategies 7
Finding the Meanings of Words:
Prior Knowledge

Skill Practice 1 *Page 99*

b. peel
c. discarded
d. spoil
e. melted
f. sinks
g. ripe
h. slice

Skill Practice 2 *Page 100*
Answers will vary. Suggested answers:

1. parts of a process
2. collect fruits and vegetables from trees, etc., when they are ready to eat
3. make something become not wet
4. the outer layers of fruits or vegetables
5. cooked over heat
6. cut into very small pieces
7. smell
8. sending something from a central location to many different locations

Reading 1
Taste – The Least Understood Sense

Connecting to the Topic *Page 101*
Answers will vary.

Previewing and Predicting *Page 101*
A
Answers will vary. Suggested answers:

1. having a good taste or flavor
2. an explanation of the biology of taste
3. an explanation of the sense of taste and how it is related to food

While You Read *Page 101*

1. There are several widespread, but incorrect, beliefs about taste buds.
2. that is, how things smell
3. not really a taste; ginger, chili, and black pepper all hurt your mouth

Reading Skill Development

Main Idea Check *Page 104*

A 3
B 5
C 7
D 2
E 4
F 6

A Closer Look *Page 104*

1. b
2. Answers will vary. Suggested answers:

TASTE	EXAMPLE FOOD
Sweet	ice cream
Sour	lemons
Salty	olives
Bitter	coffee
Umami	meat, fish, cheese, mushrooms

3. False
4. 1 c, 2 e, 3 a, 4 d, 5 b
5. d
6. True

Skill Review *Page 105*
A

1. a
2. b
3. b
4. b
5. a

B
Answers will vary.

Vocabulary Development

Definitions *Page 107*

1. identify
2. Bumps
3. Cells
4. Saliva
5. dissolve
6. Messages
7. perception
8. aspect

Words in Context *Page 107*

a. Vitamins
b. essential
c. distinct
d. protein
e. role
f. survival
g. signal
h. complex

Reading 2
Taste and Color

Connecting to the Topic *Page 109*
Answers will vary.

Previewing and Predicting *Page 109*
A

a, c. e

While You Read *Page 109*
1. These reactions to color may have helped humans survive in the past.
2. lemon-flavored; flavor was cherry
3. In contrast; much more flavor

Reading Skill Development

Main Idea Check *Page 112*

A 3	C 2
B 5	D 4

A Closer Look *Page 112*

1. b, c, d	4. a
2. True	5. d
3. b	

Skill Review *Page 113*
A

1. a	4. a
2. b	5. a
3. b	

B

1. mob	3. emotional
2. crossed out	4. strategy

Vocabulary Development

Definitions *Page 114*

1. Vision	5. appetite
2. major	6. normal
3. rotten	7. attractive
4. Reactions	8. Packaging

Word Families *Page 114*

1. reject	6. display
2. determine	7. rejection
3. display	8. determination
4. respond	9. expect
5. expectation	10. response

Skills and Strategies 8
Finding Supporting Details: Facts and Examples

Skill Practice 1 *Page 118*

1. A M
   B S
	4. A M
	   B S

2. A S
   B M
	5. A M
	   B S

3. A M
   B S
	6. A S
	   B M

Skill Practice 2 *Page 119*

1.

Example 2 Fish can taste with their skin.

Example 3 Whales can only taste salty flavors with their mouths.

2. No

Fact 1 Most humans' ability to taste is five times stronger than that of dogs.

Fact 2 Dogs get much more information from their sense of smell than their sense of taste.

Fact 3 Dogs' sense of smell is a thousand times stronger than that of humans.

3. Yes

Example 1 cows

Fact with example 1 They have to avoid eating harmful plants.

Example 2 koalas

Fact with example 2 They eat only leaves of eucalyptus trees, but they also eat only from certain individual trees.

Example 3 humans

Fact with example 3 Their sense of taste is somewhat selective, but not as much as that of animals that eat only plants.

Reading 3
Taste Preferences: Why Do Some People Hate Broccoli?

Connecting to the Topic *Page 120*
Answers will vary.

Previewing and Predicting *Page 120*
A

SECTION	TOPIC
I	Age as an explanation for differences in our sense of taste
I	Biology as an explanation for differences in our sense of taste
II	The kinds of food that competitive people prefer
I	Experience as an explanation for differences in our sense of taste
II	The kinds of food that energetic people prefer

While You Read *Page 120*
1. that is, they love to eat ice cream, cake, and other sweet food
2. People without the gene cannot detect bitterness. One gene allows some people to taste sweetness in foods with just a little bit of sugar in them.
3. If there are not many vegetables at meals, for example, children will not learn to like their taste.
4. Answers will vary. Suggested answers:
   When women are pregnant, their taste sensitivity often increases.
   And for most of us, the ability to taste decreases with age.

Reading Skill Development

Main Idea Check *Page 123*

A 5   D 6
B 4   E 3
C 2

A Closer Look *Page 123*
1. a, d
2. b, c
3. False
4. b, d
5. True
6. a S; b N; c X; d S
7. 1 c, 2 a, 3 b, 4 d

Skill Review *Page 124*
A

Answers will vary. Suggested answers:
1. a. Some people have a gene for tasting bitter foods.
   b. Some people have a gene that allows them to taste small amounts of sugar.
2. a. Exposure during pregnancy can influence a child's preferences.
   b. The foods that are served at meals during childhood can influence our preferences as adults.
3. a. Children are very sensitive to strong flavors.
   b. Women are often more sensitive to strong flavors when they are pregnant.
   c. Our senses of taste and smell become weaker as we grow older.

Vocabulary Development

Definitions *Page 125*

1. specific   5. sensitive
2. Variation   6. decline
3. pregnant   7. consistent
4. adult   8. criticize

Words in Context *Page 125*

1. competitive   5. risk
2. personality   6. requires
3. genes   7. cautious
4. individuals   8. combination

Academic Word List *Page 126*

1. adults
2. survival
3. specific
4. complex
5. variation
6. vision
7. response
8. normal
9. consistent
10. major

Exercise 2 *Page 130*

1. ABC
2. CBA
3. BAC
4. ABC
5. CAB

Making Connections

Exercise 1 *Page 129*

2. <u>Humans</u> have a good sense of smell. However, many other <u>animals</u> have a much better sense of smell.

3. One animal with a good sense of smell is the <u>rabbit</u>. <u>Dogs</u> also have a very good sense of smell.

4. <u>Age</u> is one factor that may affect your sense of smell. <u>Smoking</u> is another factor.

5. Our sense of smell gets <u>weaker with smoking</u>. However, it can also get <u>stronger with practice</u>.

6. Some people lose their <u>sense of smell</u>. When that happens, they usually lose their <u>sense of taste,</u> too.

5 Oceans

Skills and Strategies 9
Finding the Meanings of Words:
Learner Dictionaries

Skill Practice 1 *Page 133*
2. a product that you sell in another country
3. food that is grown in large amounts in order to be sold, such as the food that farmers grow
4. to travel from place to place by boat
5. the front part of a ship
6. to fall or almost fall because you hit your foot on something while you are walking or running
7. an official record of events in a journey
8. to put something somewhere and not use it until you need it

Skill Practice 2 *Page 134*
Answers will vary. These are suggestions.
2. a map of the sea
3. information that is written on paper and kept for the future
4. to catch something using a fishing net
5. to get on a boat
6. the act of giving something to someone and them giving you something else
7. to stop a boat from moving with a piece of heavy metal
8. the natural, fast movement of air

Reading 1
Oceans – An Economic Resource

Connecting to the Topic *Page 135*
Answers will vary.

Previewing and Predicting *Page 135*
A

a. F
b. T
c. T
d. T

B

b, c, e

While You Read *Page 135*
1. a) The same sentence
2. Bluefin tuna
3. a) A path
4. b) Cause something to be used for the first time

Reading Skill Development

Main Idea Check *Page 138*

A 4
B 2
C 5
D 3

A Closer Look *Page 138*
1. True
2. False
3. B → F → D → C → E → A
4. b
5. False
6. True

Skill Review *Page 139*
A

1. V
2. N
3. V
4. V
5. V
6. N

B

Answers may vary. Suggested answers:

1. to find the origin of something
2. habit or activity
3. to produce baby animals
4. to arrive somewhere
5. to grow fruit and vegetables and keep animals as a business or a way to live
6. a process which you give someone something and he or she gives you something back

Vocabulary Development

Definitions *Page 140*

1. resource
2. Oxygen
3. species
4. rapidly
5. maritime
6. Civilization
7. period
8. massive

Words in Context *Page 140*

1. century
2. quarter
3. necessities
4. goods
5. apart
6. dramatically
7. recover
8. cotton

Reading 2
The Role of Oceans in Weather and Climate

Connecting to the Topic *Page 142*
Answers will vary.

Previewing and Predicting *Page 142*
A

1. T
2. T
3. F
4. T

While You Read *Page 142*

1. a) The way something is repeated
2. oil, gas, and coal
3. floods, serious storms

Reading Skill Development

Main Idea Check *Page 145*

A 5
B 6
C 3
D 4
E 2

A Closer Look *Page 145*

1. a. W   b. C   c. W   d. C   e. W
2. a, b
3. D → B → C → E → A
4. True
5. a

Skill Review *Page 146*
A

1. connected
2. prevents something from leaving
3. becomes
4. provides the power to move something
5. a particular place or area
6. lets a gas or liquid flow out
7. the height of something in relation to the ground

B

1. spot
2. turns
3. traps
4. releases
5. drives
6. related
7. level

Vocabulary Development

Definitions *Page 148*

1. global
2. Solar
3. constantly
4. violent
5. cycle
6. permanent
7. Floods
8. Consequences

Word Families *Page 148*

1. absorb
2. evaporate
3. absorption
4. distribute
5. energy
6. evaporation
7. reversal
8. distribution
9. energize
10. reverse

Skills and Strategies 10
Finding Steps in a Process

Skill Practice 1 *Page 151*

1. How do you get from place to place in a city whose streets are made of water? In Venice, Italy, on the Adriatic Sea, you can take a *vaporetto*. It is like a bus on the water. First, you have to decide which vaporetto take. There are many different routes, so you may want to look at a map. After that, you must buy a ticket from a ticket office. Then, you need to put the ticket into a special machine. The machine writes the date and time on your ticket. You are finally ready to go to the station to wait for the next vaporetto.
2. Venice's streets of water are very beautiful. However, the city is in danger because the water is getting too high. How did this happen? First, the city was built on very soft ground. Over time, the weight of the city pushed down on the ground. This caused the city to sink. Then, sea levels started rising because of changes in the environment. Finally, water started to enter homes and businesses in Venice. Today, if there is a strong storm, up to 50 percent of the city can be covered in water.

3. One group of scientists has an interesting solution to Venice's problem: to fight water with more water. To start, the scientists will build 12 large pipes. Next, they will use the pipes to push water deep into the sand under the city. This will cause the area of sand under the city to expand. Over time, Venice will rise by as much as 12 inches (30 centimeters). In the end, the city will be safe from storms and flooding. The scientists say their plan will be cheap and effective, but other scientists are not so sure.

Skill Practice 2 *Page 152*

Answers will vary. Suggested answers:

Paragraph 1

Step 1: You have to decide which vaporetto to take.

Step 2: You must buy a ticket from the ticket office.

Step 3: You need to put the ticket into a special machine that writes the time and date.

Step 4: You are ready to go to the station to wait for the next vaporetto.

Paragraph 2

Step 1: The city was built on very soft ground.

Step 2: The weight of the city pushed down on the ground and caused the land to sink.

Step 3: Sea levels started rising because of changes in the environment.

Step 4: Water started to enter homes and businesses.

Paragraph 3

Step 1: Scientists will build 12 large pipes.

Step 2: They will use the pipes to push water deep into the sand under the city to push the sand up.

Step 3: Venice will rise by as much as 12 inches.

Step 4: The city will be safe from storms and flooding.

Reading 3
The Health of Our Oceans

Connecting to the Topic *Page 153*
Answers will vary.

Previewing and Predicting *Page 153*
A

SECTION	TOPIC
II	The effect of noise on ocean animals
III	The kinds of pollution in the oceans
I	Acid levels in the oceans
III	Where ocean garbage is located
I	The impact of acid in the oceans

While You Read *Page 153*

1. oceans
2. begins
3. Over time
4. a) Noun

Reading Skill Development

Main Idea Check *Page 156*

A	4	E	7
B	6	F	3
C	2	G	8
D	5		

A Closer Look *Page 156*

1.	b	4.	True
2.	d	5.	True
3.	b	6.	b, d, e

Skill Review *Page 157*
A

Answers will vary. Suggested answers:

1. b. Oceans absorb a lot of CO_2 every day.
   c. The CO_2 level of the oceans increases.
   d. The CO_2 combines with other chemicals to create large amounts of acid.
2. a. Toxic chemicals kill some small plants and animals.
   b. Toxic chemicals start to affect fish.
   c. The chemicals are passed on to bigger fish that eat the small fish.
   d. When we eat those fish, the chemicals enter our bodies.

B

Answers may vary. Suggested answer:
How noise pollution disrupts life in the ocean

Vocabulary Development

Definitions *Page 158*

1. Acidity
2. estimate
3. disrupt
4. dissolve
5. Pollution
6. volume
7. toxic
8. destructive

Words in Context *Page 158*

1. e
2. a
3. c
4. g
5. f
6. b
7. h
8. d

Academic Word List *Page 159*

1. dramatically
2. estimate
3. consequences
4. recover
5. release
6. distribution
7. volume
8. cycle
9. period
10. constantly

Making Connections

Exercise 1 *Page 161*

2. A large amount of oil spilled into the ocean after the
   ship sank.

3. The oil first covered the surface of the water; next, it
   reached the beach.

4. Many animals became sick after they came into
   contact with the oil.

5. The TV news reported the oil spill, and then everyone
   started talking about it.

6. Many people went to the beach to help clean up when
   they heard about the oil spill.

7. The volunteers helped clean the beach, and over time,
   the area recovered.

8. Oil spills may finally become less common, but right
   now they are a serious problem.

Exercise 2 *Page 162*

1. BAC
2. CBA
3. BAC
4. CBA
5. ACB

6 Communication

Skills and Strategies 11
Noticing Parts of Words: Noun Suffixes

Skill Practice 1 *Page 165*

1. Are you the owner of any e-books, that is, books that you download from the Internet? Each year, there are more e-books than in the past. Readers can buy e-books about any topic: math and science, sports and fitness, even entertainment. Users of e-books do not need to go to a bookstore or deal with the heaviness of printed books. In fact, researchers say that sales of printed books are going down rapidly.
2. Should companies stop making printed books, and only sell e-books? On the one hand, the production of e-books is cheap. On the other hand, many people copy and steal e-books, and companies may receive little or no payment for e-books. That is why most companies will think carefully before they take action.

Skill Practice 2 *Page 166*
Answers will vary. Suggested answers:

2. readers = people who read
3. fitness = the quality of being fit
4. entertainment = the action or process of entertaining people
5. users = people who use something
6. heaviness = the quality of being heavy or weighing a lot
7. researchers = people who do research or investigate something
8. production = the process of producing or making something
9. payment = the act of giving someone money or paying someone
10. action = the process of doing something

Reading 1
Scribes: A Tradition

Connecting to the Topic *Page 167*
Answers will vary.

Previewing and Predicting *Page 167*
A

a, c, d, f, g

While You Read *Page 167*

1. teacher
2. c) The sentence after
3. a) The same sentence
4. sender, sadness, loneliness, happiness

Reading Skill Development

Main Idea Check *Page 170*

A 3	C 4
B 5	D 2

A Closer Look *Page 170*

1. False
2. a
3. c
4. c
5. 1 d, 2 g, 3 c, 4 f,
   5 e, 6 h, 7 a, 8 b
6. b, c, d

Skill Review *Page 171*
A

1. teacher, dishwasher
2. education
3. government
4. happiness
5. decorations

Vocabulary Development

Definitions *Page 172*

1. Immigrants	5. frequent
2. records	6. Literacy
3. mechanical	7. text message
4. Functions	8. alive

Words in Context *Page 172*

1. fill out
2. cook
3. valuable
4. technology
5. post office
6. tradition
7. especially
8. documents

Reading 2
Communication in Natural Disasters

Connecting to the Topic *Page 174*
Answers will vary.

Previewing and Predicting *Page 174*
A

a, b, d, f, g

While You Read *Page 174*

1. storms, floods, or earthquakes
2. c) The sentence after
3. population
4. The Japanese earthquake and tsunami in 2011

Reading Skill Development

Main Idea Check *Page 177*

A 4
B 2
C 3
D 6
E 5

A Closer Look *Page 177*

1. a. C; b. C; c. T; d. T; e. C
2. a, b, d, f, g
3. False
4. 1 b, 2 d, 3 a, 4 c

Skill Review *Page 178*
A

2. sender
3. announcement / announcer
4. photographer
5. awareness
6. suggestion

B

1. effectiveness
2. announcement
3. photographer
4. sender
5. awareness
6. suggestions

Vocabulary Development

Definitions *Page 179*

1. earthquake
2. Victims
3. Aid
4. agency
5. Rumors
6. supply
7. Panic
8. Volunteers

Word Families *Page 179*

1. damage
2. equipment
3. information
4. equip
5. request
6. communicate
7. inform
8. communication
9. damage
10. request

Skills and Strategies 12
Finding Advantages and Disadvantages

Skill Practice 1 *Page 182*

1. Many scientists believe texting is improving our ability to communicate. One advantage of texting is it makes communication more creative. People invent new words when they text and find simple ways to explain complicated ideas. Another benefit of texting is that it helps people share information quickly and easily.

2. Some scientists believe that texting is changing students' behavior. If students often text, they may have problems in school. In fact, studies show that students who often text receive lower grades. Another negative effect of texting is that it may be making students less honest. Scientists studied the ways students communicate. They found that the students lied more often in texts than face-to-face. Why is that? The scientists explained that people are more likely to lie when they do not have to worry about their body language.

3. Texting is not only affecting our communication, but also our bodies. On the one hand, some people experience physical benefits from texting. They develop stronger, faster fingers. For example, the fastest texters in the world can type more than eight characters per second with no mistakes. On the other hand, some people have physical problems from texting too much. They lose strength in their hands, and find it difficult to hold heavy objects. Doctors call the condition "text thumb."

4. Can a simple text message make a sick person feel better? Doctors believe so. They studied patients in hospitals. They found that when patients received text messages from their family or friends, there were health benefits. Even sending a text improved the way that patients felt. Many doctors are now encouraging patients to communicate by text. For patients who cannot speak over the phone or in person, this can be a real advantage.

Skill Practice 2 *Page 183*
Answers will vary. Suggested answers:

1. a. Most people have access to text messaging on their cell phones.
   b. Texters can communicate with many people at the same time.
2. a. Drivers can send a quick message while the car is stopped.
   b. If people text while driving, even a short text can be dangerous.
3. a. Doctors and patients are communicating more often.
   b. Doctors are accidentally revealing patients' information.

Reading 3
Social Networks: How Do They Affect Our Daily Lives?

Connecting to the Topic *Page 184*
Answers will vary.

Previewing and Predicting *Page 184*
A
1. b   2. c

While You Read *Page 184*
1. users
2. a) an advantage
3. negative
4. on the other hand

Reading Skill Development

Main Idea Check *Page 187*
A 4   D 6
B 3   E 2
C 5

A Closer Look *Page 187*
1. False   5. b, d
2. False   6. True
3. c   7. c
4. b, d

Skill Review *Page 188*
A
1. 3
2. 4, 5
3. 2

B
Answers may vary. Suggested answers:

ADVANTAGES OF SNSs	DISADVANTAGES OF SNSs
SNSs are changing how we develop and maintain relationships. (Par. 2) They create a new kind of community. (Par. 2) Members of SNSs have more close relationships, get more support from others, are more politically active, and renew old relationships. (Par. 3) SNS use increases the number of relationships we have. (Par. 3)	We don't pay attention to the people we live and work with. (Par. 2) Online relationships are not as deep and permanent as face-to-face relationships. (Par. 2) Online relationships are a poor substitute for real relationships. (Par. 2) People feel worse / depressed after they use an SNS. (Par. 4) People think others have more friends, fun, and success than they do (Par. 4) SNS use creates a social distance. (Par. 5) People make fun of other SNS users. (Par. 5) SNSs make us feel small and lonely. (Par. 5)

Vocabulary Development

Definitions *Page 189*
1. Networking   5. reflect
2. enormous   6. depressed
3. concerned   7. anonymously
4. expand   8. team

Words in Context *Page 189*
1. site   5. magnify
2. billion   6. offline
3. vacation   7. interact
4. substitute   8. make fun of

Academic Word List *Page 190*

1. aid	6. enormous
2. volunteer	7. network
3. immigrant	8. document
4. depressed	9. site
5. substitute	10. tradition

Making Connections

Exercise 1 *Page 193*

1 Researchers have been studying the use of social networks in schools. On the one hand, they have found that social networks have many benefits in this context. One benefit is that students can communicate with many classmates at the same time. However, there are also negative aspects. For instance, some students use SNSs to send hateful messages or to reveal their classmates' personal information.

2 Women tend to use social networks more than men. For example, one study of Internet users in the United States found that 76 percent of women use Facebook, but just 66 percent of men do so. Why is that? One researcher gave the following explanation. Women, unlike men, tend to build relationships by sharing personal information. As a result, SNSs offer a real advantage to women.

3 Researchers say there are two types of social network users: regular users and a special group they call power users. Regular users visit social networks about once a week. In contrast, power users use social networks almost every day. They share more photos, send more messages, and request more friends to join their networks. This creates benefits for regular users. Because of power users, most social network users receive more messages than they send.

Exercise 2 *Page 194*

1. CAB	4. BAC
2. ACB	5. ABC
3. CBA	

7 Money

Skills and Strategies 13
Noticing Parts of Words: Verb Suffixes

Skill Practice 1 *Page 197*

Modern Money

How can governments modernize their systems of money? Here are three recent examples.

New Sizes

In Canada, the $5, $10, and $20 bills are all the same size. In the future, the Canadian government may change them. It may shorten some bills and lengthen others. This will help people with poor eyesight.

New Colors

For many years, all American paper money was green. That is why the color green symbolizes money to many Americans. In 2004, however, the U.S. government started to colorize U.S. dollars. The point was not to beautify the dollars but to make them harder to copy.

Different Ways to Pay

People in Sweden do not use paper money very much. Instead they use credit cards, smartphones, and computers to pay for things. Will countries like Sweden computerize all their money in the future? As governments, banks, and companies strengthen their electronic security, some countries may soon choose to simplify their economies and become cashless societies.

Skill Practice 2 *Page 198*

2. lengthen
3. symbolizes
4. colorize
5. shorten
6. simplify
7. beautify
8. strengthen
9. modernize

Reading 1
The History of Currency

Connecting to the Topic *Page 199*
Answers will vary.

Previewing and Predicting *Page 199*
A

Answers may vary. Suggested answer:
Currency

B
a, c, d

While You Read *Page 199*
1. visualize
2. specializes
3. specify
4. benefit

Reading Skill Development

Main Idea Check *Page 202*

A 4
B 3
C 5
D 2

A Closer Look *Page 202*

1. a
2. a, b
3. c
4. a, b, c, e
5. A → B → E → D → C

Skill Review *Page 203*
A

2. specialize
3. specify
4. ripen
5. theorize

B

1. theorize
2. specify
3. ripen
4. specialize
5. visualize

Vocabulary Development

Definitions *Page 204*

1. currency
2. economic
3. resolve
4. convenient
5. rare
6. dominant
7. banknote
8. electronically

Words in Context *Page 204*

1. key
2. medium of exchange
3. wallet
4. financial
5. credit card
6. barter
7. somewhat
8. forward

Reading 2
Counterfeit Money

Connecting to the Topic Page 206
Answers will vary.

Previewing and Predicting Page 206
A

Answers may vary. Suggested answer:
Banknotes

B

b, c

While You Read Page 206
1. a
2. identify
3. positive aspects

Reading Skill Development

Main Idea Check Page 209
A 4   D 3
B 5   E 6
C 2

A Closer Look Page 209
1. False   4. True
2. False   5. b
3. a, c, e   6. a

Skill Review Page 210
A

2. darken   5. brighten
3. generalize   6. realize
4. signify   7. flatten

B

1. strengthen   5. flatten
2. realize   6. brighten
3. generalize   7. signify
4. darken

Vocabulary Development

Definitions Page 211
1. Purchases   5. microscope
2. Counterfeit   6. three-dimensional
3. scanner   7. apparent
4. extremely   8. ultraviolet

Words in Context Page 211
1. features   5. treasury
2. regional   6. slightly
3. fake   7. cashier
4. handle   8. cloth

Skills and Strategies 14
Finding Causes and Effects

Skill Practice 1 Page 214

1 Espinal, in the south of Mexico, was a small town with a big problem. The economy was not growing. The reason was that people did not have enough money to pay for products and services. A local professor wanted to solve the problem, so he asked his students to create a new type of money for the town.

2 The students made a new form of money called túmin. They chose this name because it means "money" in Totonac, the local language. The creators of the túmin valued creativity. That is why each bill has a picture of Diego Rivera, a famous artist.

3 Many businesses in Espinal agreed to accept túmin. As a result, it is very popular. People there use it to buy groceries, visit the doctor, or pay for a haircut. People in Espinal like the new currency. As one café owner says, "The túmin has changed my life because it has helped me. Now, the price of things is more affordable."

Skill Practice 2 Page 214
Answers may vary. Suggested answers:
1. People did not have enough money to pay for products and services.
2. It means "money" in Totonac, the local language.
3. The creators of the túmin valued creativity.
4. It became very popular.
5. It has changed her life, and made things more affordable.

Reading 3
Money, Art, and Identity

Connecting to the Topic Page 215
Answers will vary.

Previewing and Predicting Page 215
A

SECTION	TOPIC
II	Famous buildings on paper money
I	Famous people on paper money
III	The design of the euro
I	Scenes of daily life on paper money
II	Money as an expression of national identity
II	Scenes of nature on paper money

While You Read Page 215
1. reason
2. Because
3. due to
4. That is also why

Reading Skill Development

Main Idea Check Page 218
A 4   D 5
B 6   E 2
C 3

A Closer Look Page 218
1. c
2. b
3. b
4. False
5. 1 a; 2 d; 3 b; 4 f; 5 e; 6 c

Skill Review Page 219
A
1 The picture on the Canadian five-dollar bill of children with hockey equipment is due to the sport's popularity in Canada.
2 Sometimes, bills show what is important in that country; that is why some notes show famous landmarks, such as the Petronas Towers in Malaysia, the Great Hall of the People in China, and the Bolshoi Theater in Russia.
3 Governments choose images of power plants and oil refineries so that they can highlight important aspects of their economies.

B

CAUSES	EFFECTS
Simón Bolivar was important in Venezuela's fight for independence. (Par. 2)	He appears on Venezuelan money.
China had a special political situation at the time.	In the 1960s, images of farmers and workers were very important in China. (Par. 3)
Some bills show images of ordinary people. (Par. 3)	Ordinary people seem important.
The images on the euro are representative of architecture across Europe.	The euro is able to express a shared identify for the whole region. (Par. 6)

Vocabulary Development

Definitions Page 220
1. tropical   5. responsible
2. Heroes   6. appropriate
3. Landmarks   7. Gates
4. Towers   8. Architecture

Word Families Page 220
1. replace   6. structure
2. highlight   7. refine
3. colony   8. colonize
4. refinery   9. highlight
5. replacement   10. structure

Academic Word List Page 221
1. purchase   6. appropriate
2. currency   7. apparent
3. financial   8. feature
4. highlight   9. resolve
5. structure   10. regional

Making Connections

Exercise 1 Page 223
1. Like that of the United States, the Canadian currency is called the dollar. However, Canada's dollars are very different from those of its neighbor to the south. Because Canada used to be a British colony, there is an image of Queen Elizabeth II on the front of the Canadian 20-dollar bill.

2. In 1987, Canada decided to replace its one-dollar bill with a metal coin of the same value. The government wanted a new image for the back of this coin. So it chose something familiar to most Canadians: the common loon, a type of bird that lives near water. Canadians started calling their dollars *loonies* due to the image of the loon. The name became very popular.

3. At the 2002 Winter Olympics in Salt Lake City, a worker for the Canadian national hockey team wanted to give the players good luck. So, he hid a loonie under the ice before a game. The team won that day, and both the Canadian men's and women's hockey teams went on to win gold medals. When the worker later revealed the story of the hidden coin, many Canadians were convinced that the team had won because of the "lucky loonie." As a result of that experience, the Canadian government now produces a special coin for every Olympics. The coin shows an image of the Olympics on the back.

Exercise 2 *Page 224*

1. BAC
2. ACB
3. CAB
4. BCA
5. ACB

8 Space

Skills and Strategies 15
Noticing Parts of Words: Suffixes on Adjectives

Skill Practice 1 *Page 227*

1 Some people say space exploration is a useless waste of money. However, the technology of space exploration benefits many people.
2. One advantage of space programs has been the development of satellites. Scientists use them to get information about the weather. As a result, the weather is much more predictable than it was in the past. When powerful storms happen, people know days in advance.
3. Space programs have also created important camera technology. This technology is usable in hospitals. The special cameras can look inside patients' bodies. Many medical examinations that used to be stressful for patients are now painless.
4. Because space technology is so useful here on Earth, many people believe that space programs are worth the high cost.

Skill Practice 2 *Page 228*
Answers may vary. Suggested answers:

2. able to be predicted
3. strong, full of power
4. able to be used
5. causing stress
6. without pain
7. being good for doing a task

Reading 1
Who Benefits from Space Exploration?

Connecting to the Topic *Page 229*
Answers will vary.

Previewing and Predicting *Page 229*
A
b

While You Read *Page 229*
1. countless
2. drivable
3. so
4. successful

Reading Skill Development
Main Idea Check *Page 232*
A 4   C 2
B 3

A Closer Look *Page 232*
1. False   4. a, c, d, f
2. False   5. a, b
3. b   6. b

Skill Review *Page 233*
A
1. countless   4. weightless
2. drivable   5. hopeful
3. reusable   6. successful

B
1. reusable   4. countless
2. successful   5. drivable
3. weightless   6. hopeful

Vocabulary Development
Definitions *Page 234*
1. survey   5. Planets
2. Projects   6. Gravity
3. Tires   7. Crystals
4. analyze   8. Minerals

Words in Context *Page 234*
1. vehicle   5. adapt
2. fascinate   6. program
3. crack   7. technique
4. investigate   8. Whereas

Reading 2
Living in Space

Connecting to the Topic *Page 236*
Answers will vary.

Previewing and Predicting *Page 236*
A
b, c, d, f

While You Read *Page 236*
1. a
2. a
3. reasons
4. careful
5. comfortable

Reading Skill Development

Main Idea Check *Page 239*
A 5
B 2
C 4
D 3

A Closer Look *Page 239*
1. d
2. b
3. a, b, c
4. 1 c; 2 h; 3 e; 4 f; 5 a; 6 b; 7 d; 8 g

Skill Review *Page 240*
A
2. colorful, colorless
3. fearful, fearless
4. flavorful, flavorless
5. forgetful, forgettable
6. helpful, helpless
7. powerful, powerless
8. useful, usable, useless

B
1. careful
2. colorless
3. fearful
4. flavorful
5. forgetful
6. helpless
7. powerless
8. useful or usable

Vocabulary Development

Definitions *Page 241*
1. threat
2. Challenges
3. Tubes
4. Toothpaste
5. Chefs
6. Bacteria
7. spit
8. sunrise

Words in Context *Page 241*
1. practical
2. tie
3. squeeze
4. float
5. terrible
6. rinse
7. resemble
8. lie down

Skills and Strategies 16
Finding Problems and Solutions

Skill Practice 1 *Page 244*
1. One challenge is that the tool has to be very strong but also light enough to carry into space. . . . One solution is for astronauts to protect themselves by covering tools with special blankets when they are working outside the space station.
2. There is also the problem of boredom. . . . However, modern technology is helping to improve astronauts' moods.
3. An even greater danger is that smells can change in space. . . . NASA has found an interesting solution to bad smells in space: smell tests.

Skill Practice 2 *Page 245*
1. b
2. a
3. a

Reading 3
Health Effects of Living in Space

Connecting to the Topic *Page 246*
Answers will vary.

Previewing and Predicting *Page 246*

A

SECTION	TOPIC
III	Serious health risks for astronauts
I	How astronauts feel when they first arrive at the space station
II	How astronauts feel after they return to Earth
I, II, III	The effects of living on the space station on astronauts' health

B

Answers may vary. Suggested answers:
How long astronauts stay in space
The amount of time astronauts spend in space

While You Read *Page 246*

1. a
2. effortless
3. c
4. challenge
5. resolve

Reading Skill Development

Main Idea Check *Page 249*

A 2
B 5
C 6
D 3
E 7
F 4

A Closer Look *Page 249*

1. c
2. c
3. 1 a; 2 c; 3 b; 4 d
4. d
5. d

Skill Review *Page 250*

A

Answers may vary. Suggested answers:

PROBLEM	SOLUTION
Astronauts experience space sickness.	Astronauts give themselves a few days to get accustomed to their new environment so their stomachs feel better.
Astronauts will float away when they lie down in their beds because there is low gravity in space.	Astronauts tie themselves to their beds.
Astronauts experience bone and muscle loss.	Astronauts do a lot of exercise while they are in space.
Space radiation can cause serious health problems.	Doctors monitor astronauts' health very carefully after they return to Earth.
Living in space has many health risks.	Space programs limit the amount of time that astronauts spend in space.

Vocabulary Development

Definitions *Page 251*

1. upsets
2. accustomed
3. long-term
4. circulatory
5. Muscles
6. Fluids
7. effortless
8. cancer

Word Families *Page 251*

1. adjust
2. radiation
3. contribution(s)
4. adjustment
5. monitor
6. radiate
7. balance
8. monitor
9. contribute
10. balance

Academic Word List *Page 252*

1. vehicle
2. survey
3. whereas
4. project
5. analyze
6. monitor
7. technique
8. challenge
9. contribute
10. adapt

Making Connections

Exercise 1 *Page 255*

1. In the near future, <u>astronauts may visit the planet Mars</u>. This is an exciting idea for many people. However, <u>scientists</u> must solve several problems. Their (first) challenge is to design a spaceship that can carry humans 34.8 million miles (54.7 million kilometers) from Earth to Mars. The <u>spaceship</u> will need to carry or produce a lot of fuel. It will (also) have to be made of very strong materials to survive the journey to Mars and back again.

2. (Another) problem is related to the physical and emotional condition of the <u>astronauts</u> during the journey. They will be in the spaceship for more than six months. How will they stay healthy – and happy – during the long trip? One solution could be for the astronauts to stay in a deep sleep. Some scientists are trying to develop <u>new medical technology that lowers the temperature of the human body</u>. This may allow the astronauts to stay asleep safely for weeks or even months at a time.

3. (When) they actually arrive at Mars, the <u>astronauts</u> will face (another) major challenge – the weather. Their view of Mars from space will be beautiful, (but) the weather on the planet's surface can change quickly. Powerful winds and sand storms are common. (As a result), the astronauts will need a second, smaller spaceship to land on and explore Mars.

Exercise 2 *Page 256*

1. BAC
2. CAB
3. ACB
4. BCA
5. CAB

Quizzes

Reading Quiz · Units 1 and 2

Read the passage. Then answer the questions that follow.

Memory Myths

Imagine this scene. The man in the front of a room may be responsible for a terrible crime. A woman is explaining what she saw. She says she saw the man with a gun. She saw him shoot the gun and kill another man. The man says he didn't do it. He says he was not there, but the woman says she is sure this is the right man. She remembers him very clearly.   1

Who is right? Whom should we believe? We usually believe people when they report what they have seen, especially a crime. We believe them because we think that memories are reliable. But are memories really reliable? Or is this just a myth?   2

Myth: Human memory is like a video camera that records events as they happen. After memories are recorded in the brain, they cannot be changed.   3

Fact: Human memories are more like pieces of a puzzle that we put together as a record of something we have seen or heard. We remember only parts of the event. Even more important, our memories can change. We forget parts of past events, and we also often add details to our memories. You could be talking about something that happened to you, for example, a car accident. Then someone suggests a detail about the accident. You may begin to include that detail in your memory even if it did not really happen. Our memories are not always reliable records of events as they happened.

Myth: Our memories fade gradually over time.   4

Fact: We actually forget most of what happens quite quickly. One expert claims that we forget about 40 percent of what happens to us after about 20 minutes.

Myth: When a person is very confident about a memory, this is a good indication that   5
the memory is accurate.

Fact: Confidence is not an indication of accuracy. For example, older people are generally more certain about their memories than younger people. Yet, their memories are less reliable. Also, people often become more confident about their memory of an event over time. However, during this same period, they often forget details of that event.

Myth: Experts can help people get lost memories back by asking questions about   6
the event.

Fact: In general, we cannot recover memories that we have lost. When experts or the police begin to ask questions, this can change memories or even create false memories that never really happened.

Understanding these myths and facts about memory is important. It is especially   7
important to understand that the memories of eyewitnesses, that is, people who see crimes, are not always accurate or reliable. Many people have spent a long time in prison based on a report of an eyewitness. Later, some of these reports turn out to be wrong.

Reading Quiz · Units 1 and 2 (continued)

A Main Idea Check

1. What is the main idea of the whole reading? (5 points)
   a. We forget a lot of what happens to us every day.
   b. Our memories are not always accurate.
   c. You should not believe eyewitnesses.

2. Match each paragraph main idea below to a paragraph from the reading. Write the number of the paragraph on the blank line. (5 points)

   _____ If someone is confident about a memory, it does not mean the memory is accurate.

   _____ We forget events quite quickly.

   _____ When a memory is lost, it is gone forever.

B A Closer Look
Look back at the reading to answer the following questions. (2 points each)

1. The human brain records events as they happen. **True or False?**

2. According to the reading, what is one way that your memory can change after an event has already happened?
   a. You begin to remember more things about the event.
   b. Someone else suggests something about that event.
   c. You become less confident.

3. We forget almost half of what happens to us after about 20 minutes. **True or False?**

4. According to the reading, which group of people is most confident about their memories?
   a. older people   c. people who have seen a crime
   b. the police   d. well-educated people

5. What may happen if people answer questions about an event in the past?
   a. They will forget more slowly.
   b. They may remember more about the event.
   c. They may create false memories.

C Definitions
Find words in the reading that can complete the following definitions. (2 points each)

1. If something is _____ , you can believe it and trust it. (*adj*) Par. 2

2. When something _____ , it becomes weaker. (*v*) Par. 4

3. When something happens _____ , it happens slowly, a little bit at a time. (*adv*) Par. 4

4. If you are _____ about something, you are sure about it. (*adj*) Par. 5

5. A / An _____ is a sign or signal that makes something clear. (*n*) Par. 5

Vocabulary Quiz · Units 1 and 2

Unit 1

A The words in the box are words that you studied in Unit 1. Choose the best word to complete each sentence. You will not use all the words. (2 points each)

accomplish	detect	gap	postpone	punishment	rude
assignment	due	instant	prefer	reward	support

1. This library book was _____ three weeks ago.

2. You need to find more _____ for the ideas in your paper.

3. The book was a / an _____ success. It sold a million copies in just one month.

4. We could _____ a strong smell of smoke after the fire.

5. I need to finish my history _____. I have to give it to my teacher tomorrow morning.

6. In many cultures, it is _____ to chew your food with an open mouth.

7. I _____ to cook my own food. I don't like to go to restaurants.

8. We worked hard, but unfortunately, we did not _____ very much.

B Circle the letter of the best word to complete each sentence. The answer is always an Academic Word List word from the unit. (2 points each)

1. The students who worked hard were able to _____ good grades for the whole year.
   a. advise   b. maintain   c. access   d. consult

2. I always try to consider different _____ before I make a decision.
   a. rewards   b. tasks   c. images   d. perspectives

3. We feel very _____ and hopeful about the future.
   a. positive   b. logical   c. guilty   d. rude

4. The mayor announced that the next _____ for the city is to improve education.
   a. task   b. impact   c. advice   d. access

5. Safety was the most important _____ in the decision to close schools during the storm.
   a. task   b. gap   c. benefit   d. factor

6. Research has shown that stress can have a _____ effect on memory.
   a. recent   b. negative   c. primary   d. visual

7. The new professor is a / an _____ in the field of chemical engineering.
   a. research   b. factor   c. expert   d. consultation

Vocabulary Quiz (continued)

Unit 2

A The words in the box are words that you studied in Unit 2. Choose the best word to complete each sentence. You will not use all the words. (2 points each)

ancient	curiosity	handsome	made up	originated	prove
collection	familiar	immediately	mermaid	profit	resist

1. I think my neighbor took some flowers from my garden, but I cannot _____ it.

2. The restaurant is five years old, but this is the first year it will make a / an _____ .

3. His face is very _____ , but I cannot remember where I have seen him before.

4. The _____ of paintings at this museum is famous all over the world.

5. The little girl _____ a story about a princess and a horse.

6. If you feel a pain in your chest, you should call your doctor _____ .

7. Historians believe the first coffee trees were in Ethiopia, whereas tea _____ in China.

8. Today he is an old man with gray hair, but when he was young, he was very _____ .

B Circle the letter of the best word to complete each sentence. The answer is always an Academic Word List word from the unit. (2 points each)

1. The new hospital will be _____ for everyone who lives in the city.
   a. intentional   b. beneficial   c. familiar   d. relevant

2. The university was _____ in the early eighteenth century.
   a. published   b. assisted   c. established   d. traced

3. My grandfather never _____ to anyone where he hid all of his money.
   a. abandoned   b. occurred   c. created   d. revealed

4. The report provides _____ that the world has become hotter.
   a. assistance   b. evidence   c. generation   d. deception

5. Changes in the law had a / an _____ impact across the country.
   a. familiar   b. relevant   c. widespread   d. intentional

6. The _____ of the Internet changed how people communicate.
   a. benefit   b. creation   c. repetition   d. virus

7. Several people ran to _____ a woman who fell down in the street.
   a. assist   b. persist   c. occur   d. trace

Skills and Strategies Quiz · Units 1 and 2

Unit 1

A Skills and Strategies 1: Finding the Meanings of Words: Definitions
Answer the following questions about Skills and Strategies 1. (2 points each)
Choose two answers to complete each sentence.

1. Writers sometimes explain the meaning of words they use. They use phrases such as _____ *is* and _____ *other words* and then provide the meaning of the word.
   a. in   b. means   c. that   d. this

2. Writers may also signal the definition of a word with punctuation like _____ or _____ .
   a. ( )   b. !   c. ;   d. –

Read the following paragraph and answer the questions that follow.

   Your behavior when you were a child may be related to your success later in life. A famous psychology experiment from the 1970s showed this in a very simple way. Scientists gave the children in the experiment a choice. The children could get one piece of candy right away. Or, if they could delay – wait for – the candy, they could have two pieces. The scientists studied the children again many years later. They found that the children who needed *instant gratification*, that is, something good right away, were less successful when they became adults.

3. Find two signals of definitions. Highlight them.

4. If you *delay* something, you do it later. **True or False?**

5. If you need *instant gratification*, you probably finish your work before you do something fun like watching a movie or playing a game. **True or False?**

B Skills and Strategies 2: Finding the Topic of a Paragraph
Answer the following questions about Skills and Strategies 2. (2 points each)

1. Most paragraphs are about one topic. **True or False?**

2. The topic of each paragraph always appears in the first sentence. **True or False?**

3. One way to guess the topic of a paragraph is to look for words that appear more than once. **True or False?**

Read the following paragraph and answer the questions that follow.

   Making decisions is a complicated process. When we make decisions, we use two different systems in the brain. The first system is good for solving problems. It is slow, thoughtful, and careful. However, most decisions require quick action. For these decisions, we use the other system. It is much faster. It relies on feeling instead of thinking. Experts say we use this system much more often than the first one.

4. What clue(s) can you use to find the topic of the paragraph?
   a. the last sentence   b. a summary   c. key terms   d. the first sentence

5. Highlight a phrase that gives the topic of the paragraph.

Unit 2

A Skills and Strategies 3: Finding the Meaning of Words: Examples
Answer the following questions about Skills and Strategies 3. (2 points each)

1. Writers sometimes explain the meaning of words by giving examples. Which of the following are signals of examples? Circle two answers.

   a. therefore   b. such as   c. like   d. in other words

2. Lists often contain examples that can help you understand the meaning of a word.
   True or False?

Read the following paragraph and answer the questions that follow.

   Rumors often include interesting stories. Some are true, but usually they are not. For example, maybe you hear a story about someone you know. You are not sure if it is true, but you tell your friend about it. Your friend tells his friend. Soon the rumor is everywhere. Rumors about celebrities, like musicians, movie stars, and politicians, are very common. For many years there has been a rumor that President Obama was not born in the United States, but it is just a rumor. It is not true.

3. Highlight signals of examples.

4. *Rumors* are never true. **True or False?**

5. A *celebrity* is a famous person. **True or False?**

B Skills and Strategies 4: Finding the Main Idea of a Paragraph
Answer the following questions about Skills and Strategies 4. (2 points each)

1. The topic and the main idea of a paragraph are the same thing. **True or False?**

2. The main idea is usually in the last sentence in the paragraph. **True or False?**

3. The main idea is what the writer wants to say about the topic. **True or False?**

Read the following paragraph and follow the instructions.

   There are many myths about what happens in the brain. Many people continue to believe them although scientific research has proven that they are not true. These myths include general, but important, ideas. For example, most people believe that we make good decisions when we rely on our first reactions. Other myths are about less important things. For example, many people believe that if someone is looking at the back of your head, you will sense it. Both ideas are wrong.

4. Underline the topic of the paragraph.

5. Highlight the main idea of the paragraph.

Reading Quiz · Units 3 and 4

Read the passage. Then answer the questions that follow.

The Fifth Taste

For a long time, scientists thought there were four different types of taste: sweet, sour, salty, and bitter. That changed in the early twentieth century. A Japanese chemistry professor, Kikunae Ikeda, wanted to know why sometimes his soup was more delicious than other times. He discovered that the difference was in seaweed, a plant that grows in the ocean, which his wife sometimes put in his soup. It gave the soup a special, delicious flavor.

1

Ikeda identified the chemical in the seaweed that gave the soup this special flavor. The chemical's name is *glutamate*. He called this flavor *umami*, which means "delicious flavor." Glutamate occurs naturally in meat, some kinds of fish and cheese, tomatoes and mushrooms, and other foods. Glutamate can also be added to food. It can improve the taste of foods that do not have a lot of their own flavor.

2

Ikeda made a pure form of glutamate, called *monosodium glutamate* – or MSG. He understood that this product could make a lot of money so he started a company. That company became Ajinomoto, a large Japanese food company. It makes more than U.S. $12 billion every year! The company began by selling MSG in Asia. Cooks at home and in restaurants loved the product because it made their food taste so good. The company and the product became very successful.

3

Outside of Asia, however, Ajinomoto and MSG were not as familiar. Most people tried it for the first time when they went to Chinese restaurants. They enjoyed the flavor of the food. Then, in 1968, some people began to complain that they felt weak or sick after they ate in Chinese restaurants. Others said they got headaches. People said the MSG was the cause of their reactions although they had eaten MSG for many years without problems. Soon, more and more people reported these reactions. Customers began to demand food without MSG.

4

Because of these reports, the popularity of MSG began to fall. Scientists have not been able to find a clear connection between MSG and health problems. However, some people continue to complain about its effects. Sometimes beliefs are more powerful than science. Public feeling about MSG became very negative. Many people did not want to buy food with MSG.

5

Then everything changed again at the beginning of the twenty-first century. Food lovers began to rediscover the fifth taste. But they used the same name that Ikeda had used – umami. All over the world, famous chefs in expensive restaurants began to describe the flavors in their food as "umami." Everyone wanted to taste food with umami flavor. A restaurant called Umami Burger opened in Los Angeles. The owner said his hamburgers were the most delicious in the world. When an Umami Burger restaurant opened in New York, people waited for three hours for a table. And so the fifth taste left the name *MSG* behind and began a new and successful life as umami.

6

Reading Quiz · Units 3 and 4 (continued)

A Main Idea Check

1. What is the main idea of the whole reading? (5 points)
   a. The discovery of the fifth taste has had a significant impact in science.
   b. Some people like the fifth taste a lot, whereas others don't like it at all.
   c. The success and popularity of food with the fifth taste has gone up and down.

2. Match each paragraph main idea below to a paragraph from the reading. Write the number of the paragraph on the blank line. (5 points)

   _____ The fifth taste became popular again with the name *umami*.

   _____ MSG became very popular and successful in Asia.

   _____ Some people began to report health problems and blamed them on MSG.

B A Closer Look
Look back at the reading to answer the following questions. (2 points each)

1. What gives food the umami flavor?
   a. soup
   b. meat
   c. a chemical

2. Why was Ajinomoto's MSG so successful?
   a. It improved the flavor of food.
   b. It was very pure.
   c. It was very good for making Asian food.

3. Choose the correct answer to complete the sentence.
   MSG became unpopular because some people _____.
   a. knew it was from seaweed   c. didn't like the flavor
   b. believed it made them sick   d. said it was only for Asian food

4. Scientists showed that MSG has caused serious health problems. **True or False?**

5. MSG gives food an umami flavor. **True or False?**

C Definitions
Find words in the reading that can complete the following definitions. (2 points each)

1. When something is _____, it is not mixed with anything else. (*adj*) Par. 3

2. To _____ is to say that something is not good enough – that you are not satisfied with it. (*v*) Par. 4

3. A / An _____ is a feeling or action in response to something else. (*n*) Par. 4

4. _____ means how much people enjoy or like something. (*n*) Par. 5

5. A / An _____ is someone who cooks in a restaurant. (*n*) Par. 6

Vocabulary Quiz · Units 3 and 4

Unit 3

A The words in the box are words that you studied in Unit 3. Choose the best word to complete each sentence. You will not use all the words. (2 points each)

crossed out	envious	fundamental	mob	profitable	regular
effective	figures	lack	population	reduce	sign

1. The _____ on the door said, "Do not enter."

2. The _____ of Los Angeles is about 10 million.

3. I _____ each task on my list after I finished it.

4. The medicine was very _____. He felt better an hour after he took it.

5. She was very _____ when her sister got a new car. She wanted a new car, too.

6. Many people have left the village because of the _____ of jobs there. There is more opportunity in the city.

7. The doctor told him to _____ the amount of sugar and sweet food that he eats.

8. The sales _____ for smartphones have been increasing every year.

B Circle the letter of the best word to complete each sentence. The answer is always an Academic Word List word from the unit. (2 points each)

1. Businesses use television and newspaper advertising to _____ their products.
   a. design   b. achieve   c. perform   d. promote

2. The _____ of the new program is to increase the number of students who go to college.
   a. method   b. goal   c. item   d. awareness

3. The exclamation point (!) is a common _____ for danger.
   a. item   b. principle   c. symbol   d. emotion

4. If two products are very _____, you should buy the one that is less expensive.
   a. similar   b. rational   c. fundamental   d. aware

5. People from the _____ met to discuss plans for a new school.
   a. principle   b. community   c. military   d. population

6. Different products require different advertising _____ to increase their sales.
   a. symbols   b. values   c. bargains   d. strategies

7. It is important to consult a medical _____ if you have serious health problems.
   a. customer   b. professional   c. strategy   d. community

Vocabulary Quiz (continued)

Unit 4

A The words in the box are words that you studied in Unit 4. Choose the best word to complete each sentence. You will not use all the words. (2 points each)

appetite	combinations	distinct	message	rejected	sensitive
attractive	criticized	essential	personalities	ripe	signal

1. She left a / an _____ on the refrigerator door. It said she would be home at 8:00.

2. The two sisters have very different _____; one is confident, the other is always scared of everything.

3. This dress looks very _____ on you. I think you should buy it.

4. I burned my hand last week. It is getting better, but the skin is still very _____ .

5. The newspaper strongly _____ the president's plan for the economy.

6. I ate too much at lunch. Now I don't have any _____ for dinner.

7. The apple tasted sour because it was not _____ yet.

8. The other members of my group didn't like my idea for the project. They _____ it right away.

B Circle the letter of the best word to complete each sentence. The answer is always an Academic Word List word from the unit. (2 points each)

1. This is a very _____ and difficult problem, so it will take a long time to solve.
   a. competitive   b. specific   c. complex   d. distinct

2. The _____ reason for their decision to leave the country was the safety of their family.
   a. normal   b. major   c. cautious   d. sensitive

3. There was an angry _____ to the recent tax increase.
   a. reaction   b. determination   c. aspect   d. signal

4. Fortunately, the number of people who lost their jobs _____ this year.
   a. declined   b. displayed   c. rejected   d. criticized

5. After _____ to very cold temperatures during the night, my car often will not start.
   a. variation   b. perception   c. exposure   d. expectation

6. Travel to another country _____ a passport.
   a. requires   b. displays   c. responds   d. determines

7. If we can _____ the problem, we will be able to repair the camera.
   a. reject   b. expect   c. require   d. identify

Skills and Strategies Quiz · Units 3 and 4

Unit 3

A Skills and Strategies 5: Finding the Meanings of Words: Contrast
Answer the following questions about Skills and Strategies 5. (2 points each)

1. Writers sometimes explain the meaning of words by showing contrasts. Which of the following are signals of contrast? Circle two answers.

   a. that is
   b. unlike
   c. however
   d. such

2. Which word in the sentence is in contrast to the word *identical*?
   This computer software can tell the difference between images that look identical.

   a. images
   b. difference
   c. software
   d. look

Read the following paragraph and answer the questions that follow.

   The weather has a major effect on what people buy. Some connections are obvious. When it is warm, people buy more juice and cold drinks. In contrast, when the temperature drops, stores sell more soup. However, other connections are not so easy to see. If the day is cloudy and gray, people spend less money, but when the weather is fair, people will spend more for the same thing. One study showed that people were willing to spend 37 percent more on tea after sitting in the sunlight.

3. Highlight the signals of contrast in the paragraph.

4. Something that is *obvious* is clear and easy to understand. **True or False?**

5. When the weather is *fair*, you should bring an umbrella. **True or False?**

B Skills and Strategies 6: Finding the Topic and Main Idea of a Reading
Answer the following questions about Skills and Strategies 6. (2 points each)

1. You can usually find the main idea of the reading in the first paragraph. **True or False?**

2. You can usually find something about the topic of the reading in every paragraph. **True or False?**

3. One way to describe the main idea is as _____.
   a. the most important thing about the topic
   b. the writer's opinion
   c. what the writer wants to say about the topic
   d. how to describe all the paragraphs

4. The main idea of a reading includes its topic. **True or False?**

5. The writer often restates the main idea of a reading in the first paragraph. **True or False?**

Skills and Strategies Quiz (continued)

Unit 4

A Skills and Strategies 7: Finding the Meanings of Words: Prior Knowledge
Answer the following questions about Skills and Strategies 7. (2 points each)

1. The best way to handle words that you don't know is to look up each one in the dictionary.
   True or False?

2. You can often guess the meaning of a word you don't know if you know all of the other words in the sentence. **True or False?**

Read the following paragraph. Use your prior knowledge and clues in the context to answer the questions that follow.

Most animals can taste, but not all animals can taste the same things. Humans have lots of taste buds – about 10,000. Herbivores, such as cows and rabbits, need even more taste buds because of their diet. They need to be able to taste the difference between plants that are good for them and plants that could be bad for them. They need to know if the plants contain toxins that could make them sick or even kill them.

3. An animal's *diet* is _____ .
   a. the sense of taste   c. its health
   b. what it eats   d. how it acts

4. An *herbivore* only eats plants. **True or False?**

5. *Toxins* help plants and animals to grow. **True or False?**

B Skills and Strategies 8: Finding Supporting Details: Facts and Examples
Answer the following questions about Skills and Strategies 8. (2 points each)

1. A main idea requires support. **True or False?**

2. What are some common forms of support? Circle two answers.
   a. examples   b. definitions   c. people   d. facts

3. Where is the best place to look for support for the main idea?
   a. in the first sentence
   b. in the middle of the paragraph
   c. in the last sentence

Read the following paragraph and follow the instructions.

There are several different conditions that can change our sense of taste. For example, temperature can affect how bitter or salty something tastes. Your fork or spoon can also make a difference. Some kinds of metal make foods taste more salty. One of the most important factors, however, is memory. Research studies have shown that if you eat something when you are having a good time, the next time you eat it, it will taste better!

4. Highlight the signals of support.

5. Underline the support for the main idea.

Reading Quiz · Units 5 and 6

Read the passage. Then answer the questions that follow.

Communicating Under Water

Humans use all five senses to communicate and to understand the world around   1
them. However, we rely most on our hearing and on our vision, that is, our ability to see.
Other animals, dogs for example, rely more on their sense of smell. These senses work
well on land, but what about in the water? How do animals in the ocean, such as whales,
dolphins, and fish, communicate and understand their environment?

The senses work differently in water. Vision does not work as well under water. Light   2
makes it possible for animals to see on land. Light travels easily through air but not
through water. As a result, most of the ocean is somewhat dark. It is difficult to see things
clearly. Hearing is much more reliable. Sound moves quickly through the water, five
times faster than through the air. It also can travel much farther than on land.

Many animals in the ocean use sound to communicate and to understand their   3
environment. They use sound in several different ways. *Echolocation* is one of them. This
is how echolocation works: When animals make a sound, the sound hits objects in the
environment, such as rocks, sand, or other animals. Animals can hear it when the sound
hits these different objects. They use this information to figure out their location. It also
helps them figure out what else is in the environment. This process allows the animals to
find food or family members and to escape from their enemies. Whales and dolphins use
echolocation. Many fish use sound in a different way. They make sounds as a warning
to others about enemies that are nearby. They use other sounds to try to scare these
enemies away.

Sound is essential for communication in the ocean. Animals rely on their hearing   4
to survive. Unfortunately, the ocean is becoming louder. Human activity has increased
the variety and level of sound in the ocean. All of this noise can confuse animals. It
makes their communication and echolocation less reliable. This can create dangerous
conditions for many animals. They cannot be sure of their own location or the location
of friends, enemies, or food. It is also difficult for them to communicate accurately.

Ocean animals communicate easily and well in the water. In contrast, humans have   5
to rely on technology for underwater communication. On land, most communication
across long distances uses radio signals. The Internet and cell phones both use radio
waves to send messages. However, radio signals do not travel well through water. As a
result, most human communication across the ocean today goes through cables – thick,
heavy wires. Scientists and engineers are trying to find new ways to send messages
through the water without these cables.

Reading Quiz · Units 5 and 6 (continued)

A Main Idea Check

1. What is the main idea of the whole reading? (5 points)
   a. Sound is important for underwater animal communication.
   b. Many animals use echolocation to communicate and survive.
   c. Soon humans may be able to use the Internet under the ocean.

2. Match each paragraph main idea below to a paragraph from the reading. Write the number of the paragraph on the blank line. (5 points)

   _____ Humans are making communication more difficult for animals in the ocean.

   _____ Ocean animals use sound in different ways and for different purposes.

   _____ Sound is effective for communication under water.

B A Closer Look

Look back at the reading to answer the following questions. (2 points each)

1. Which of these does *not* explain why hearing works better than vision under water?
   a. Sound travels quickly under water. c. Sounds are louder under water.
   b. Sound travels farther under water. d. Light does not travel well through water.

2. How do animals use echolocation in the ocean? Circle all that apply.
   a. to scare away their enemies
   b. to understand their own location
   c. to find food
   d. to warn others

3. Fish communicate with echolocation. **True or False?**

4. Choose the correct answers to complete the sentence.
   Human activity makes it difficult for ocean animals to _____ and _____.
   a. breathe   c. move quickly
   b. find food   d. communicate

5. Scientists do not need cables to use the Internet underwater. **True or False?**

C Definitions

Find words in the reading that can complete the following definitions. (2 points each)

1. To _____ something _____ is to understand it or find the answer. (*2-word verb*) Par. 3

2. Your _____ is where you are. (*n*) Par. 3

3. To _____ is to get away from. (*v*) Par. 3

4. If something _____ you, it makes you feel uncertain. (*v*) Par. 4

5. When you do something _____, you do it correctly with no mistakes. (*adv*) Par. 4

Name: _____   Date: _____

Vocabulary Quiz · Units 5 and 6

Unit 5

A The words in the box are words that you studied in Unit 5. Choose the best word to complete each sentence. You will not use all the words. (2 points each)

absorbs	destructive	floods	oxygen	pollution	toxic
cotton	evaporates	massive	permanent	solar	violent

1. Heavy storms last week caused _____ in two towns near the river.

2. We are trying some new ideas. If they are successful, we will make them _____.

3. Chemicals from the factory outside of the city are causing serious water _____.

4. When you breathe, you take _____ into your lungs.

5. A lot of clothes that we wear are made from _____.

6. When it rains, the ground _____ most of the water.

7. The sun releases a / an _____ amount of energy – enough for 2,880 trillion lights!

8. Some sea animals produce chemicals that are _____ to humans. Be careful what you eat!

B Circle the letter of the best word to complete each sentence. The answer is always an Academic Word List word from the unit. (2 points each)

1. If you want to become a doctor, it will require a long _____ of study and training.
   a. quarter   b. period   c. volume   d. level

2. The ocean's currents never stop; they are _____ moving.
   a. dramatically   b. reverse   c. rapidly   d. constantly

3. It took the city at least five years to _____ from the storm.
   a. recover   b. distribute   c. release   d. disrupt

4. Smoking can have very serious _____ for your health.
   a. consequences   b. resources   c. absorption   d. distribution

5. Scientists _____ that the world's temperature has risen almost one degree Celsius since 1880.
   a. reverse   b. disrupt   c. estimate   d. distribute

6. Water is one of our most important natural _____.
   a. organisms   b. cycles   c. consequences   d. resources

7. The _____ of water in the ocean is very large – more than 300,000 cubic miles (1,230,000 cubic kilometers).
   a. evaporation   b. energy   c. volume   d. reversal

 Making Connections Intro

Vocabulary Quiz (continued)

Unit 6

A The words in the box are words that you studied in Unit 6. Choose the best word to complete each sentence. You will not use all the words. (2 points each)

agency	equipment	frequent	magnified	request	valuable
damage	fill out	literacy	panic	rumors	victim

1. You should not believe those _____ that you hear. They are not true.

2. This painting is very _____. You should take better care of it.

3. When several banks closed, there was a _____. Customers were afraid they would lose their money.

4. Thunderstorms are most _____ during the summer months.

5. If you want to apply for the program, you will need to _____ these three forms.

6. Some of the _____ at the factory is very old and often breaks down.

7. South Korea has a very high _____ rate. About 98 percent of the population can read.

8. Recent events have _____ the importance of the elections next year.

B Circle the letter of the best word to complete each sentence. The answer is always an Academic Word List word from the unit. (2 points each)

1. _____ leave their home countries for many different reasons.
   a. Teams   b. Volunteers   c. Records   d. Immigrants

2. It is important to carry your personal _____ with you when you travel to another country.
   a. documents   b. functions   c. equipment   d. agency

3. The football stadium is _____. It can hold 200,000 people.
   a. depressed   b. mechanical   c. enormous   d. valuable

4. I just tried a new product that is a / an _____ for sugar. It is sweet but has no calories.
   a. function   b. substitute   c. tradition   d. request

5. The town was very small 10 years ago, but it has _____ significantly since then.
   a. interacted   b. communicated   c. equipped   d. expanded

6. A _____ of experts arrived yesterday. They will help the city plan for the future.
   a. tradition   b. team   c. substitute   d. technology

7. Several countries sent _____ after an earthquake destroyed half of the city.
   a. aid   b. functions   c. communication   d. immigrants

Skills and Strategies Quiz · Units 5 and 6

Unit 5

A Skills and Strategies 9: Learner Dictionaries
Answer the following questions about Skills and Strategies 9. (2 points each)

1. When should you use a dictionary to find the meaning of a word? Circle all that apply.
   a. if it is important for understanding the reading
   b. if you have never seen the word before
   c. if you cannot figure out the meaning from context

2. What can help you choose the correct definition in a learner dictionary? Circle all that apply.
   a. part of speech   c. rules
   b. meaning   d. example sentences

Read the following paragraph and answer the questions that follow.

   Humans are taking too many fish out of the ocean. This is called overfishing. Sadly, we are eating the fish faster than they can **reproduce**. Experts say that about 85 percent of fish species that we eat are in danger of disappearing. Large ocean fish, like tuna, are in the biggest danger. We need to **address** this problem immediately.

3. Which definition of *reproduce* fits the word in the paragraph?
   a. to produce a young animal or plant; to have babies   b. to copy

4. Which part of speech matches the use of *address* in the paragraph?
   a. noun   b. verb

5. Which meaning matches the use of *address* in the paragraph?
   a. (*v*) try to solve   b. (*v*) make a speech

B Skills and Strategies 10: Steps in a Process
Answer the following questions about Skills and Strategies 10. (2 points each; 4 points for question 4)

1. Which of the following words or phrases signal steps in a process? Circle three answers.
   a. finally   b. in the beginning   c. so   d. next

2. Process descriptions usually follow _____ order.
   a. space   b. time   c. place   d. rank

Read the following paragraph and answer the questions that follow.

   The Arctic Ocean is covered with ice for most of the year. At the beginning of the year the sea is frozen, but every summer the ice starts to melt. After that, the sun hits the dark ocean instead of bright ice. So, the ocean absorbs more sunlight and heat. Then the water temperature rises. By the end of the summer, much of the sea ice has melted.

3. Highlight the words and phrases that signal steps in a process.

4. Put these events in the correct order.
   a. The ocean absorbs sunlight.   c. The sunlight hits the ocean.
   b. The ocean gets warmer.   d. The sea ice begins to melt.

Skills and Strategies Quiz (continued)

Unit 6

A Skills and Strategies 11: Noticing Parts of Words – Noun Suffixes
Answer the following questions about Skills and Strategies 11. (2 points each)

1. A *suffix* appears at the end of a word. **True or False?**

2. Which of the following are suffixes that mark nouns? Circle three answers.
   a. *-tion*   b. *-less*   c. *-ment*   d. *-ness*   e. *-able*

3. Which of the following suffixes can you add to a verb to make a noun? Circle
   three answers.
   a. *–ly*   b. *-er*   c. *-or*   d. *-ness*

Read the following paragraph and follow the instructions.

The interaction between patients and doctors is very important. When you are sick, it is essential for you to understand both your illness and your treatment, so your doctor should explain things clearly. Perhaps most important, however, is for the doctor to be a good listener.

4. Highlight four words with noun suffixes.

5. List their root words.

B Skills and Strategies 12: Finding Advantages and Disadvantages
Answer the following questions about Skills and Strategies 12. (2 points each)

1. Which words are signals of advantages and disadvantages? Circle three answers.
   a. positive   b. benefit   c. however   d. negative   e. therefore

2. Which phrases may indicate that the author is going to *compare* advantages
   and disadvantages?
   a. sometimes   b. on the other hand   c. as a result   d. unlike

Read the following paragraph and answer the questions that follow.

Before babies learn to talk, they can learn to communicate by making signs with their hands. Parents say that babies benefit from the use of hand signs because they can express their needs clearly. The parents say that this system has an advantage for them, too. Instead of listening to their baby scream, parents can immediately understand why the baby is unhappy. Some people believe there is a negative side to this idea. They say that children who use hand signs are slower in learning to talk, but there is no evidence that this is really true.

3. Highlight words that signal advantages.

4. Underline a word that signals a disadvantage.

5. Using hand signs with babies has more advantages than disadvantages. **True or False?**

Reading Quiz · Units 7 and 8

Read the passage. Then answer the questions that follow.

How to Buy a Cup of Coffee on the Moon

If you travel to New York, you need to bring dollars. To buy a cup of coffee in Paris, you will need euros. For Tokyo, come with yen. What if you want to buy a cup of coffee on the moon? How will you pay? That sounds like a crazy question, but some companies started thinking about the answer several years ago.   1

Travelex is a company that exchanges currency for businesses and travelers. In 2007, the company introduced a new currency for use in space, called QUID. When it appeared in 2007, one QUID was worth about US $12.50. QUID is not made of paper like dollars or euros. Instead, QUIDs are coins made of strong plastic. Travelex says this is the best material for use in space. The same plastic is used in spaceships, so the company knows it is tough. The coins have no sharp edges, so they are safe. They cannot hurt anyone if they float away in the low-gravity environment.   2

Many experts believe that space tourism will expand significantly in the near future. They also say that the price of space travel will drop. Travelex says that space tourists will need QUIDs to pay for things. For example, travelers could use QUIDs to pay for a room at a space hotel.   3

But will the space tourists of the future really use coins like QUIDs? It is unlikely that tourists of the future will carry a wallet full of money when they visit the moon or Mars. Even on Earth today, cash and coins are disappearing. Many people pay for everything with a credit card or a cell phone. Or, they pay over the Internet. Business experts predict that very soon we may have a "cashless" economy. In other words, we will not have to carry real money. So, was QUID a serious idea? Maybe not.   4

Nevertheless, the idea of money in space is serious. One company that helped begin the move to a cashless economy is PayPal. PayPal began in 1998. The company created a system that lets customers pay online without a credit card. Leaders at PayPal believe that soon people will need a way to pay for things while they are traveling in space. However, they don't believe that these travelers will use coins, like QUIDs. Instead, travelers will need a cashless system like PayPal.   5

In 2013, the company began a new program called *PayPal Galactic*. The goal of PayPal Galactic is to serve the space tourists of the future. It will connect them to their money back on Earth. *Apollo* astronaut Buzz Aldrin likes the idea. He says, "Whether it's paying a bill . . . or helping a family member on Earth, we'll need access to money." So, someday soon, perhaps you will be able to buy that cup of coffee on the moon.   6

Reading Quiz · Units 7 and 8 (continued)

A Main Idea Check

1. What is the main idea of the whole reading? (5 points)
    a. Traveling in space will be expensive and have a lot of challenges.
    b. Several companies have been thinking about how people will pay for things in space.
    c. Systems for payment in space will probably be very similar to payment systems on Earth.

2. Match each paragraph main idea below to a paragraph from the reading. Write the number of the paragraph on the blank line. (5 points)

    _____ On Earth we are moving toward a cashless economy.

    _____ Travelex believes space travelers will need their own currency.

    _____ PayPal believes that payments in space will not require cash or currency.

B A Closer Look
Look back at the reading to answer the following questions. (2 points each)

1. Choose two items below to complete the sentence:
    QUIDs are _____ and made of _____ .
    a. paper   c. sharp
    b. plastic   d. round

2. The price of space travel will probably go down. **True or False?**

3. It is likely that space travelers will use cash. **True or False?**

4. On Earth, a lot more people are using _____ to pay for things than in the past.
    a. cash
    b. phones
    c. QUIDs

5. *PayPal allows people to pay for things using _____ .*
    a. a credit card   c. the Internet
    b. QUIDs   d. coins

C Definitions
Find words in the reading that can complete the following definitions. (2 points each)

1. To _____ is to change one thing for another thing with a similar value. (*v*) Par. 2

2. If something is _____, it is strong and does not break easily. (*adj*) Par. 2

3. The _____ of something is its side or farthest point. (*n*) Par. 2

4. If something is _____, it probably will not happen. (*adj*) Par. 4

5. _____ is money in the form of bills and coins. (*n*) Par. 4

Vocabulary Quiz · Units 7 and 8

Unit 7

A The words in the box are words that you studied in Unit 7. Choose the best word to complete each sentence. You will not use all the words. (2 points each)

architecture	credit card	hero	key	microscope	responsible
convenient	extremely	highlight	landmark	rare	wallet

1. He did not bring any money so he paid for the dinner with his _____ .

2. The weather in California has been _____ dry. Last year there was almost no rain.

3. Scientists need a / an _____ to examine the organisms because they are so small.

4. The most famous _____ in Paris is the Eiffel Tower.

5. The doctor said her disease is very _____ . He had never seen it before.

6. As a manager, she is _____ for the work of the whole office.

7. Living in the city is very _____ . Stores and transportation are nearby.

8. She carries pictures of her grandchildren in her _____ .

B Circle the letter of the best word to complete each sentence. The answer is always an Academic Word List word from the unit. (2 points each)

1. English is the _____ language among scientists and engineers.
   a. apparent   b. economic   c. dominant   d. regional

2. The tallest human-made _____ in the world is Burj Khalifa, a building in Dubai.
   a. gate   b. feature   c. currency   d. structure

3. The United States _____ more oil every year than any other country in the world.
   a. specializes   b. refines   c. highlights   d. resolves

4. I put all of my _____ into one bag so that I could carry them more easily.
   a. wallets   b. replacements   c. features   d. purchases

5. Venezuela's most remarkable geographic _____ is Angel Falls, a waterfall that is 3,212 feet (almost 1,000 meters) high.
   a. feature   b. currency   c. tower   d. architecture

6. The teacher told the children to try to _____ their own problems before asking for help.
   a. replace   b. specify   c. resolve   d. refine

7. The _____ situation is beginning to improve. More people are getting good jobs.
   a. key   b. dominant   c. apparent   d. economic

Vocabulary Quiz (continued)

Unit 8

A The words in the box are words that you studied in Unit 8. Choose the best word to complete each sentence. You will not use all the words. (2 points each)

bacteria	cancer	crack	float	resemble	threat
balance	contribute	effortless	practical	sunrise	upset

1. I am going to repair the _____ in the wall before it gets bigger.

2. We can see the _____ every morning from the bedroom window.

3. He didn't tell his mother that he failed the test because he knew the news would _____ her.

4. Everyone says that I _____ my mother more than my father.

5. Effort and intelligence both _____ to a student's success.

6. Scientists are still searching for a cure for some types of _____ .

7. Inside the national park, wild animals are a / an _____ to tourists. They can be very dangerous.

8. It is sometimes difficult to _____ your job and family responsibilities.

B Circle the letter of the best word to complete each sentence. The answer is always an Academic Word List word from the unit. (2 points each)

1. Her doctors are using a new _____ to help improve her breathing.
   a. mineral   b. contribution   c. project   d. technique

2. The children quickly _____ to their new school and made lots of friends.
   a. analyzed   b. adjusted   c. contributed   d. resembled

3. My car was stolen last night. The police have promised to _____ the crime.
   a. investigate   b. monitor   c. adapt   d. balance

4. Each of the children did a _____ about a different planet.
   a. survey   b. project   c. technique   d. challenge

5. Cars and factories both _____ to the problem of air pollution.
   a. generalize   b. adjust   c. adapt   d. contribute

6. A police _____ has been parked in front of my house since morning.
   a. program   b. monitor   c. vehicle   d. project

7. A _____ of customers showed that most people prefer to shop early in the morning.
   a. technique   b. survey   c. challenge   d. balance

Skills and Strategies Quiz · Units 7 and 8

Unit 7

A Skills and Strategies 13: Noticing Parts of Words – Verb Suffixes
Answer the following questions about Skills and Strategies 13. (2 points each)

1. Which of the following are suffixes that mark verbs? Circle three answers.

   a. *-en*   b. *-less*   c. *-ify*   d. *-ize*   e. *-able*

2. What part of speech does adding the suffix *-en* create?

   a. noun   b. verb   c. adjective

3. What do the suffixes *-en* and *-ify* mean?

   a. to be like or similar to   c. to make or cause to be
   b. to be full of

Read the following paragraph and answer the questions that follow.

   I always tell people that credit cards are great. Using a credit card simplifies shopping because I don't have to bring money with me. It also lengthens the time I have before I need to pay for what I buy. I bought a television last month, and I don't have to pay until next month! I really like that part, but I should clarify one important thing. Credit cards can also create problems. It is so easy to spend money with them that I sometimes spend too much!

4. Highlight three words with verb suffixes.

5. Which of the following are root words? Circle two answers.

   a. strengthen   b. pure   c. class   d. apologize

B Skills and Strategies 14: Finding Causes and Effects
Answer the following questions about Skills and Strategies 14. (2 points each)

1. Which words and phrases are signals of cause? Circle two answers.

   a. reason   b. due to   c. as a result   d. therefore

2. Which words and phrases are signals of effect? Circle two answers.

   a. therefore   b. due to   c. in any case   d. so

3. Another word for *effect* is *result*. **True or False?**

Read the following paragraph and follow the instructions.

   Inflation is a situation in which prices keep going up. One week milk costs two dollars and a few weeks later, it costs three dollars, then four dollars. Why does this happen? One reason is that people feel good about their future, and so they are willing to spend more money. This makes stores raise prices because they know people will pay. Costs can also have an effect on prices. A business may have to pay more for materials or pay its workers more. As a result, the business will have to increase the price of its products.

4. Highlight signals of causes.

5. Underline signals of effects.

Unit 8

A Skills and Strategies 15: Noticing Parts of Words – Adjective Suffixes
Answer the following questions about Skills and Strategies 15. (2 points each)

1. Which of the following are suffixes that mark adjectives? Circle two answers.
   a. *-able*   b. *-ful*   c. *-ify*   d. *-ment*   e. *-less*

2. What part of speech does adding the suffix *-ful* create?
   a. nouns   b. verbs   c. adjectives

3. What does the suffix *-less* mean?
   a. similar to   b. full of   c. without

Read the following paragraph and answer the questions that follow.

The space program has given us all sorts of useful technology. Some we use every day. Perhaps you use a wireless telephone or computer. The technology for those products began in the space program. There are other common products that you may not think of when you think about space, for example, car tires. Technology that was developed for space travel makes the tires you use on Earth more reliable.

4. Highlight three words with adjective suffixes.

5. What is the root of the word *reliable*?

B Skills and Strategies 16: Finding Problems and Solutions
Answer the following questions about Skills and Strategies 16. (2 points each)

1. Which words are signals of problems? Circle three answers.
   a. danger   b. difficulty   c. resolve   d. challenge

2. Which words are signals of solutions? Circle two answers.
   a. improve   b. resolve   c. in any case   d. so

3. Writers usually present problems before solutions. **True or False?**

Read the following paragraph and follow the instructions.

The United States space agency, NASA, is famous for facing challenges and solving problems. Some businesses are trying to improve their performance by using NASA's methods. NASA follows these steps: First, identify the problem. Then, think of several different ways to resolve it. Finally, consider the consequences of each of these solutions.

4. Highlight signals of problems.

5. Underline signals of solutions.

Skills and Strategies Quiz (continued)

Name: ___ Date: ___

Making Connections Intro   ©Copyright Cambridge University Press 2016 **Photocopiable**   63

Quizzes Answer Key

Units 1 and 2

Reading Quiz – Units 1 and 2

A Main Idea Check
1. b   2. 5, 4, 6

B A Closer Look
1. False   3. True   5. c
2. b   4. a

C Definitions
1. reliable   4. confident
2. fades   5. indication
3. gradually

Vocabulary Quiz – Units 1 and 2

Unit 1

A

1. due   5. assignment
2. support   6. rude
3. instant   7. prefer
4. detect   8. accomplish

B

1. b   3. a   5. d   7. c
2. d   4. a   6. b

Unit 2

A

1. prove   5. made up
2. profit   6. immediately
3. familiar   7. originated
4. collection   8. handsome

B

1. b   3. d   5. c   7. a
2. c   4. b   6. b

Skills and Strategies Quiz – Units 1 and 2

Unit 1

A

1. c, a
2. a, d
3. Your behavior when you were a child may be related to your success later in life. A famous psychology experiment from the 1970s showed this in a very simple way. Scientists gave the children in the experiment a choice. The children could get one piece of candy right away. Or, if they could delay – wait for – the candy, they could have two pieces. The scientists studied the children again many years later.

They found that the children who needed instant gratification, that is, something good right away, were less successful when they became adults.
4. True
5. False

B

1. True
2. False
3. True
4. c, d
5. Making decisions is a complicated process. When we make decisions, we use two different systems in the brain. The first system is good for solving problems. It is slow, thoughtful, and careful. However, most decisions require quick action. For these decisions we use the other system. It is much faster. It relies on feeling instead of thinking. Experts say we use this system much more often than the first one.

Unit 2

A

1. b, c
2. True
3. Rumors often include interesting stories. Some are true, but usually they are not. For example, maybe you hear a story about someone you know. You are not sure if it is true, but you tell your friend about it. Your friend tells his friend. Soon the rumor is everywhere. Rumors about celebrities, like musicians, movie stars, and politicians, are very common. For many years there has been a rumor that President Obama was not born in the United States, but it is just a rumor. It is not true.
4. False
5. True

B

1. False
2. False
3. True
4. and 5. There are many myths about what happens in the brain. Many people continue to believe them although scientific research has proven that they are not true. These myths include general, but important, ideas. For example, most people believe that we make good decisions when we rely on our first reactions. Other myths are about less important things. For example, many people believe that if someone is looking at the back of your head, you will sense it. Both ideas are wrong.

Units 3 and 4

Reading Quiz – Units 3 and 4

A Main Idea Check
1. c   2. 6, 3, 4

B A Closer Look
1. c   3. b   5. True
2. a   4. False

C Definitions
1. pure   4. Popularity
2. complain   5. chef
3. reaction

Vocabulary Quiz – Units 3 and 4

Unit 3

A
1. sign   5. envious
2. population 6. lack
3. crossed out 7. reduce
4. effective   8. figures

B
1. d   3. c   5. b   7. b
2. b   4. a   6. d

Unit 4
A
1. message   5. criticized
2. personalities 6. appetite
3. attractive   7. ripe
4. sensitive   8. rejected

B
1. c   3. a   5. c   7. d
2. b   4. a   6. a

Skills and Strategies Quiz - Units 3 and 4

Unit 3
A
1. b, c
2. b
3. The weather has a major effect on what people buy. Some connections are obvious. When it is warm, people buy more juice and cold drinks. In contrast, when the temperature drops, stores sell more soup. However, other connections are not so easy to see. If the day is cloudy and gray, people spend less money,

but when the weather is fair, people will spend more for the same thing. One study showed that people were willing to spend 37 percent more on tea after sitting in the sunlight.
4. True
5. False

B
1. True   3. c   5. False
2. True   4. True

Unit 4
A
1. True   3. b   5. False
2. True   4. True

B
1. True
2. a, d
3. b
4. and 5. There are several different conditions that can change our sense of taste. For example, temperature can affect how bitter or salty something tastes. Your fork or spoon can also make a difference. Some kinds of metal make foods taste more salty. One of the most important factors, however, is memory. Research studies have shown that if you eat something when you are having a good time, the next time you eat it, it will taste better!

Units 5 and 6

Reading Quiz – Units 5 and 6

A Main Idea Check
1. a   2. 4, 3, 2

B A Closer Look
1. c   3. False   5. False
2. b, c   4. b, d

C Definitions
1. figure out 4. confuses
2. location   5. accurately
3. escape

Vocabulary Quiz – Units 5 and 6

Unit 5
A
1. floods   5. cotton
2. permanent   6. absorbs
3. pollution   7. massive
4. oxygen   8. toxic

B

1. b   3. a   5. c   7. c
2. d   4. a   6. d

Unit 6

A

1. rumors   5. fill out
2. valuable   6. equipment
3. panic   7. literacy
4. frequent   8. magnified

B

1. d   3. c   5. d   7. a
2. a   4. b   6. b

Skills and Strategies Quiz – Units 5 and 6

Unit 5

A

1. a, c   3. a   5. a
2. a, d   4. b

B

1. a, b, d
2. b
3. The Arctic Ocean is covered with ice for most of the year. At the beginning of the year the sea is frozen, but every summer the ice starts to melt. After that, the sun hits the dark ocean instead of bright ice. So, the ocean absorbs more sunlight and heat. Then the water temperature rises. By the end of the summer, much of the sea ice has melted.
4. d, c, a, b

Unit 6

A

1. True
2. a, c, d
3. b, c, d
4. The interaction between patients and doctors is very important. When you are sick, it is essential for you to understand both your illness and your treatment, so your doctor should explain things clearly. Perhaps most important, however, is for the doctor to be a good listener.
5. interact, ill, treat, listen

B

1. a, b, d
2. b, d
3. and 4.   Before babies learn to talk, they can learn to communicate by making signs with their hands. Parents say that babies benefit from the use of hand signs because they can express their needs clearly. The parents say that this system has an advantage for them, too. Instead of listening to their baby scream, parents can immediately understand why the baby is unhappy. Some people believe there is a negative side to this idea. They say that children who use hand signs are slower in learning to talk, but there is no evidence that this is really true.
5. True

Reading Quiz – Units 7 and 8

A Main Idea Check

1. b   2. 4, 2, 5

B A Closer Look

1. d, b   3. False   5. c
2. True   4. b

C Definitions

1. exchange   4. unlikely
2. tough   5. Cash
3. edge

Vocabulary Quiz – Units 7 and 8

Unit 7

A

1. credit card   5. rare
2. extremely   6. responsible
3. microscope   7. convenient
4. landmark   8. wallet

B

1. c   3. b   5. a   7. d
2. d   4. d   6. c

Unit 8

A

1. crack   5. contribute
2. sunrise   6. cancer
3. upset   7. threat
4. resemble   8. balance

B

1. d	**3.** a	**5.** d	**7.** b
2. b	**4.** b	**6.** c	

Skills and Strategies Quiz – Units 7 and 8

Unit 7

A

1. a, c, d

2. b

3. c

4. I always tell people that credit cards are great. Using a credit card simplifies shopping because I don't have to bring money with me. It also lengthens the time I have before I need to pay. I bought a television last month, and I don't have to pay until next month! I really like that part, but I should clarify one important thing. Credit cards can also create problems. It is so easy to spend money with them that I sometimes spend too much!

5. b, c

B

1. a, b

2. a, d

3. True

4. and 5. *Inflation* is a situation in which prices keep going up. One week milk costs two dollars and a few weeks later, it costs three dollars, then four dollars. Why does this happen? One reason is that people feel good about their future, and so they are willing to spend more money. This makes stores raise prices because they know people will pay. Costs can also have an effect on prices. A business may have to pay more for materials or pay its workers more. As a result, the business will have to increase the price of its products.

Unit 8

A

1. a, b, e

2. c

3. c

4. The space program has given us all sorts of useful technology. Some we use every day. Perhaps you use a wireless telephone or computer. The technology for those products began in the space program. There are other common products that you may not think of when you think about space, for example, car tires. Technology that was developed for space travel makes the tires you use on Earth more reliable.

5. rely

B

1. a, b, d

2. a, b

3. True

4. and 5. The United States space agency, NASA, is famous for facing challenges and solving problems. Some businesses are trying to improve their performance by using NASA's methods. NASA follows these steps: First, identify the problem. Then, think of several different ways to resolve it. Finally, consider the consequences of each of these solutions.